The Voices of Silence:
Meditations on T. S. Eliot's *Four Quartets*

The Rev. J. C. Woods

Createspace.com

Cover Photo: St John the Evangelist, Little Gidding, copyright to John Salmon and licensed for reuse under Creative Commons #TL1281

Burnt Norton Pools from Maddery@blogspot.com
Eliot Memorial from EastCoker.com/tseliot.html
Notre Dame de la Garde Marseilles from globeimage.net

ISBN: 1480097594
Createspace.com

Of a rose, a lovely rose
Of a rose is all my song.

Harken to me both old and young.
How this rose began to spring;
A fairer rose to my liking
            In all the world I ne know none.

Five branches of that rose there been,
The which be both fair and sheen;
The rose is called Mary, heaven's queen.
            Out of her bosom a blossom sprang.

The first branch was of great honour:
That blessed Mary should bear the flower,
There came an angel from heaven's tower
            To break the devil's bond.

The second branch was great of might,
That sprang upon Christmas night,
The star shone above Bethlehem bright,
That man should see it both day and night.

The third branch did spring and spread:
Three kings then the branch gan led
Unto our Lady in her child bed:
Into Bethlehem that branch sprang right.

The fourth branch it sprang to hell,
The devil's power for to fell:
That no soul therein should dwell,
            The branch so blessedfully sprang.

The fifth branch it was so sweet,
It sprang to heaven, both crop and root.
Therein to dwell and be our Bote:
            So blessedly it sprang.

Pray we to her with great honour,
She that bare the blessed flower.
To be our help and our succor,
            And shield us from the fiendes bond. (15th Century English)

For Elise

On the occasion of our Thirtieth Wedding Anniversary

Contents

Preface

Eliot . . . . brought into consciousness, and into confrontation with one another, two opposite things: the spiritually negative character of the contemporary world and the spiritually positive character of past tradition. He was obsessed with time. The past and modern coexist in his poetry as an imagined present of conflicting symbols to which are attached values of spiritual life or death. Although he had in his mind very vivid pictures of the past, he never saw the past as a nostalgic world into which he could escape from the present. He always saw it as a force still surviving within the present which could be brought into life and action. And he derived from Dante, and placed at the center of his picture of the contemporary world, the idea of a life not bound by its pastness or its presentness: but the same always in being outside any particular time (though very consciously placed within it) and related to what he called "final facts" and the supernatural.[1]

Eliot's question may be stated succinctly: how are we to understand our "presence" in time? His method of answering this question is, by modern standards, controversial. A philosopher (Heidegger) taking on the same question answered it by phenomenological analysis. Eliot, though trained as a philosopher, sought his answer, not in philosophy, but in poetry. His answer, as another philosophical poet put it, is "unscientific,"[2] and, in the Modern age, everything unscientific is heresy.

*   *   *

Philosophy and poetry differ categorically as philosophy orders and directs the mental manipulation of symbols, while poetry attempts, through manipulating symbols, to change the behavior of bodies in space. One orders thought, the other feeling. One appeals to the mind, the other to the will. Logic teaches us to think more efficiently, but a poem seduces us to vice or to virtue. Philosophy tries to explicate existence conceptually, assuming a congruence between reality and

9

symbolic representations. Poetry assumes symbols cannot directly model reality, bringing the world into language requires technical trickery. Philosophy attempts to view reality objectively, as if we could see it "out the window." Poetry attempts, in light of the impossibility of such a view, to examine our common feelings about reality. The ancient struggle between poetry and philosophy (Plato, Republic, 10.607b) is sourced in the poets' refusal to "say the thing straight out," based on a prior denial that it is *possible* to "say the thing straight out." Eliot aims to write "philosophical poetry," bringing philosophical precision to rhythm and rhyme.

* * *

The struggle between heart and mind revolves around self-explanation. This is the mind's primary function, constantly exhausting itself striving to explain *itself to itself*. The heart, on the other hand, reaches out in desire. Mind becomes impatient: if the heart cannot *explain* its desires, it *should* surrender them in favor of what the mind, by its analysis, finds good. The heart remains resolutely unconvinced and loves what it loves without needing to say why.

The struggle is familiar to the readers of another philosophical poet, Dante. The Inferno begins with the pilgrim (as opposed to Dante who narrates the story) limping, dragging his left foot (Inferno 1.30). This symbolizes his initial moral state: his mind (right foot) engaged, but his will (left foot) derelict. He does not do the good he knows. To know the good and not to *do* it is to be damned by one's own knowledge. Inferno and Purgatorio have as their project reforming the pilgrim's will and healing his limp.

* * *

Dante, in the Middle Ages, did not experience the fragmentation we face today. Dante's world was completely sensual: if the stars appeared to move and the Earth to stand still, then medieval science worked (quite cleverly) to confirm that point of view. Humans were only beginning to extend their senses artificially (Dante, growing older, wore an early pair of reading glasses). The West's love affair with technology was in its infancy (Dante's is the earliest depiction we have of a chiming clock (Paradiso 10.139-144)). Today, so much of what we know about the world is technologically mediated and mathematically based that we are constantly recalling (the modern equivalent to *Memento mori?*) that our senses mislead us.

When a science based on falsifying the senses becomes the arbiter of what is "true," we lose a basic trust in the world. We still *say* "sunrise" and "sunset" (describing our sensual experience), but, on reflection, *know* our eyes play us false: the sun neither "rises" nor "sets" in relation to a horizon that is an optical illusion caused by the curvature of the earth. Modern people daily endure more psychic dissonance than a medieval person could have borne in a lifetime (when Siger of Brabant merely *suggested* an idea seen to be true from one angle could be seen as false from another, Thomas Aquinas was *not* amused.).[3]

*   *   *

Don't get me wrong: I have no problem with falsifying the senses so long as we take responsible precautions. Socrates argued philosophy in the marketplace, where all could hear. Plato, with his execution fresh in mind, withdrew philosophy into the Academy, out of the public's earshot: the original "ivory tower" built to protect philosophers by muffling their conversations. Christianity, derided as "Platonism of the people,"[4] falsified the sensual world by the claim of a real world (the kingdom of heaven) of which Dante was the Lewis and Clark.

Until recently, science took Socrates' example seriously – avoiding the blame for destabilizing society by withdrawing from the public square or bewildering the uninitiated with allegory. Modern science has led to the broad airing of destabilizing truths and the canonization of loud mouths as secular saints (I am thinking of Galileo who, having pointed a telescope at Jupiter, could not keep continence). This in the name of the public's right to know, a right unheard of in war or diplomacy nor even in science when research is funded for a proprietary end.

*   *   *

Human life is so sudden and uncertain that normal functioning requires a constant forgetting, ameliorating or explaining. This has historically been the role of religion, but even here the sciences have intruded showing, in a pluralistic world, that no religion offers the definitive meaning of the world, but only doctrinal formulations incompatible with and contradictory to all the others. This would be no problem if science offered a coherent account of the world:

In the end, there would be no new Christian "world-picture" to replace the medieval conception of God, man, and world after the scientific revolution. But neither would a secular one emerge. It is not true, as many historians and even philosophers would have it, that we now take our bearings from a new picture of the cosmos that emerged from the new sciences. We have never lived in a Copernican, or Newtonian, or Darwinian, or Einsteinian world. The fact that we can draw up such a list proves the point: we have lost "the world," if by world we mean the natural "whole" that Greeks and Christians once thought linked God and man. Instead, modern man lives with an ever-changing string of hypotheses about the cosmos and must resign himself to the fact that whatever picture he finds adequate today will probably be found inadequate tomorrow.[5]

*   *   *

Dante, as the most accessible expositor of the "medieval conception of God, man, and world," can explain (or rather, have Beatrice explain as we eavesdrop) *why* the stars move. All creation is imprinted with the image (logos) of the Divine Poet, the image of its goal and perfection. All things, animate or inanimate, mindless or sentient, are drawn, instinctively, to their place in that image. Lower subsistences (minerals, plants and animals) follow instinct blindly. The higher minds (Angels and

12

Humans), possessing free will, must consciously perceive the pattern in their natures to follow It (Paradiso 1.103-141). The stars are driven, in their imperfection, by their desire for perfection, the yearning to become one with their Creator who is the goal of their being.

How does Modern science explain the stars' motion? It tells us they move because they were, already, in motion (inertia). How did they come to be in motion? Was there some first mover who set them in motion? And if so, was it more than the first in a series of identical events, infinitely regressive like the final digit of pi? Science refuses, on principle, to answer such questions.

* * *

Dante's contemporary, William of Occam (he of the razor), took the first step toward the disenchantment of science in his "principle of parsimony." Every boy learns the principle his first day on the baseball diamond: never throw a "live" baseball except to stop an advancing runner or assist a put out because each throw risks errancy. Here the thrown baseball is analogous to the positing of explanatory principles. The explanation accounting for the most data in the fewest steps is to be preferred as each additional step risks a misstep.

Based on this principle, scientific explanation became simpler, less ambitious in it aims. It need not explain, as did Dante and the Schoolmen, the whole, but only local phenomena. Dante and the Schoolmen had to fit all things into a universal schema. William let modern science off that hook.

* * *

While still at school our children get taught that water <u>consists</u> of the gases hydrogen and oxygen . . . . Anyone who doesn't understand is stupid. The most important questions are concealed.[6]

A concealed question is: how can you combine two atoms of a substance that is gaseous at room temperature (hydrogen) with an atom of a substance that is gaseous at room

13

temperature (oxygen), and derive a substance that is *liquid* at room temperature (H_2O)?

The scientific community imposes its understanding of water on everyone by means of its formulas and definitions, which I want to characterize as abstract. We find it possible, in other words, to speak of water in terms of a standard table of elements, and this is called the scientific concept of water. One might want to agree that water <u>in the abstract</u> consists of hydrogen and oxygen, bearing in mind of course, that water in the abstract does not exist. In the abstract, or at the furthest remove from our senses, water is always the same thing, but in existence water is endlessly varied and on the move. The contrast between abstraction and existent becomes overwhelming if you compare the scientific account of water with the enormous variety of things we observe about an existing body of water such as the Niagara River. The actual river is individuated by the shape of its bed, its quantum of free oxygen, the types of life it supports, its level of contamination, and on and on.[7]

Scientific reductionism produces a concept simpler than the existing things it represents. The concept water (H_2O) differs in mode from any existing water (whether liquid, solid or vapor). The Ancient and Medievals expended great energy attempting to account for this distinction. Modern science passes over it in silence. In his poem, Eliot attempts to fill this gap by referring to conceptions philosophical and religious, Western and Eastern, rendering the sense of the world as a mysterious whole that science neglects by abstraction.

*   *   *

If Modern Science has brought psychical dislocation in its train, its claim to fame is its staggering success on the physical plane. Never have so many souls, at any one time and, perhaps through all time, peopled the earth, nor have they ever had access to so much knowledge. This was no accident of history, but a self-conscious project:

For they (the sciences) opened my eyes to the possibility of gaining knowledge, which would be very useful in life, and of discovering a practical philosophy which might replace the speculative philosophy taught in the schools. Through this philosophy we could know the power and action of fire, water, air, the stars, the heavens and all the other bodies in our environment, as distinctly as we know the various crafts of our artisans; and we could use this knowledge – as our artisans use theirs -- for all the purposes for which it is appropriate, and thus make ourselves, the lords and masters of Nature. This is desirable not only for the invention of innumerable devices which would facilitate our enjoyment of the fruits of the earth and all the goods we find there, but also, and most importantly, maintenance of health, which is undoubtedly the chief good, and the foundation of all other good in this life.[8]

The modern age began with a conscious decision to tack philosophy into a different wind, philosophy no longer beginning in wonder at the mystery of the universe (Plato, Theaetetus 155d), but with doubting the senses, experimentally determining whether what we see and feel is real. Science makes an autopsy of nature in the hope of mastering it.

The project succeeded beyond its progenitors' dreams. In prior ages, the earth managed human populations by plague and famine with the occasional assist of beastly human beings. We, moderns, taking hold of our destiny, dominate the earth as no earlier people. But if we expected, entering our glory, our science to usher in a Golden Age, we find, instead, an exploding human population intensifying the struggle among peoples and tribes for scarce resources. What, to the few million humans of prior centuries seemed a limitless bounty, seems to us, in our billions, scant.

This scarcity was exacerbated when the leading nations of the industrial revolution began enslaving and stealing the resources of the less advanced peoples to fuel their technological advance. Colonialism and imperialism poisoned the well of globalism leading to our current "arms race" of third world industrialization. In the century of my birth all the nasties hatched out in wars of all against all. Technology, through abundance, has taught us to know scarcity in new and frightening ways.

*   *   *

15

World War II provides the historical backdrop for Four Quartets. All of them (except Burnt Norton, published in 1936) were written and published during the war (East Coker 1940, Dry Salvages 1941, Little Gidding 1942). They are not martial poems, nor are they jingoistic, but their sales during the war indicate that the English, huddled in their air raid shelters, found them a comfort.[9] War, though not the essential image of the poem, provided its refining crucible. The poem is about self-transformation: the Eliot who ends the poem is not the Eliot who began it.

*   *   *

The most cursory reader knows that bad writers outnumber good. It is, moreover, true that good writers, on occasion, compose bad books. Certainly, an engaging style and a cracking plot can keep us turning pages despite a verbal "heartburn," just as a trip to McDonald's can be an agreeable experience grease be damned. But bad writing, like burgers and fries, do not build up, but only build out.

Good writing, like good architecture, has an organic relation between plan and function. Plato gave the canonical definition:

Every speech must be put together like a living creature, with a body of its own; it must be neither without head nor without legs; and it must have a middle and extremities that are fitting both to one another and to the whole work. (Phaedrus 264c)

that is to say, good writing expresses a complete and integral thought without conflicting with its mode of expression. As even so small a defect as a limp may fatally flaw an animal, so a book must also be fitted to survive its environment.

*   *   *

As a child, my favorite poet's last play was entitled, "What use are Flowers?" As she and Eliot died within a week of each other (though she was of a younger generation) their plays

16

concerned like questions. Like the Wasteland, which describes Western culture blown to smithereens, her play considered a nuclear holocaust and an old hermit who, discovering a child, takes it upon himself to explain human culture in hope that something will survive. The prospects are bleak, but the attempt necessary.

We see a beautiful painting or hear a symphony and need not be told that they have been authored. We all feel the impulse of beauty, and the urge, with what technique we possess and however imperfectly, to model the image outwardly. This feeling is, of course, the source of the teleological argument for God's existence: we see beauty and assume design and a designer because that is how we are made.

*   *   *

Economics is often derided as the "dismal science," but aesthetics is gloomier still. We can think quantity, but quality, eluding thought, may fade to a ghostly abstraction. This is especially galling when technological, thinking types, unable to turn "beauty" into a concept conflate "beauty" and "the pleasing," polluting love's river with all manner of foulness.

That poetry's first function is to please goes without saying. The poet pleases by articulating *feelings* we lacked words to express. Poetry pleases by self-recognition, by the 'aha' moment when the poem unties the knot of inward mystery. The poem not only resolves my confusion, but tells me it was not unique, that another (the poet) before me stood pondering direction at this very same crossroads.

*   *   *

In considering Eliot's method, we begin with his title, Four Quartets. Are the four poems actually one poem? Not really: they never appeared together until each had had separate publication.[10] Each is capable of standing alone:

I should like to indicate, that these poems are all in a particular set form which I had elaborated, and the word "quartet" does seem to

me to start people on the right tack for understanding them ("sonata"
in any case is <u>too</u> musical). It suggests to me the notion of making a
poem by weaving in together three or four superficially unrelated
themes: the "poem" being the degree of success in making a new whole
out of them.[11]

Eliot's explanation operates on two levels, describing
both the internal structure of the individual poems and how they
(to the extent Eliot has been successful) form a single poem.

*   *   *

A long poem's *shape* is its means to coherence. The most
usual form of the long poem is the epic in which character and
plot bind the poem in a continuous narrative. Eliot's long poem
has no plot and he (or rather, fragments of himself) is the only
character. Thus, sonota-form, a musical and not a narrative
shape, solves the problem of coherence.

*   *   *

A "quartet" is a piece of music in which four instruments
develop themes in conversation and, in the end, return to the
key in which they began to repeat the initial theme, wiser for the
effort.

Eliot attempts to explicate the relation of time to timeless
moments. Time unfolds musically, as life unfolds. Life, like a
symphony, is sonata-form. Motifs echo each other, themes
develop, all leading to a recapitulation and resolution. But, life is
not simply musical flow: there are also *moments*, within the flow,
that transcend it; moments in which we become aware of the
reality of the whole. In these moments, time ceases its flow
becoming *oceanic* in that we experience, not the single moment,
but the *weight* of all moments at once. Wittgenstein, perhaps,
said it best:

If we take eternity to mean not infinite temporal duration but
timelessness, then eternal life belongs to those who live in the present.
Our life has no end in just the way in which our visual field has no
limits.[12]

18

*   *   *

But what can Eliot mean in speaking of a poem as "music," and what is his aim in so doing?

It may appear strange, that when I profess to be talking about the 'music' of poetry, I put such emphasis upon conversation. But I would remind you, first, that the music of poetry is not something that exists apart from the meaning. Otherwise, we could have poetry of great musical beauty which made no sense, and I have never come across such poetry. The apparent exceptions only show a difference of degree: there are poems in which we are moved by the music and take the sense for granted, just as there are poems in which we attend to the sense and are moved by the music without noticing it.[13]

Here Eliot gives us an entrance into the "music" of poetry: it, unlike prose, is sound as well as sense. Speaking of their shared vocation, the ghost of poetic tradition says:

Since our concern was speech, and speech impelled us
  To purify the dialect of the tribe
  And urge the mind to aftersight and foresight, (LG II.127-129)

Poetry, unlike prose and like music, has a *body*. Translate prose into a different language and, so long as you accurately convey the meaning, you lose nothing essential. But translating a poem is akin to vivisection: the sounds the words make are its body and to exchange them for others does violence. Even if we can maintain the meter, the rhyme <u>and</u> the thought, the poem is still, irreducibly, the sound of its words.

Poetry, unlike prose, must be *heard*. It is not meant merely to convey information: a written poem, like a musical score, implies *performance*. So the transcription of a poem, like the script of a play or the score of a sonata, exists to allow its repetition.

*   *   *

We enter a new realm of dialectic when we self-consciously distinguish poetry and prose: silence-word, male-female, soul-body, technology-nature, eternal-temporal. The

19

Quartets begin in Burnt Norton with Eliot one-sidedly affirming soul over body, eternity over temporality, male over female (it is perhaps his saving grace that he values poetry over prose: this leads him to value nature over technology and we are off to the races). The Dry Salvages breaks with the original pattern, championing nature over technology. This crescendos in his prayer to the Blessed Virgin, culminating in dual theophanies: female and male. It ends with a balance of male and female wisdom in the Fourteenth Century mystics Dame Julian of Norwich and the author of the Cloud of Unknowing.

The first poem (Burnt Norton), written before the war, manifests the uncontrolled masculine principle. The wartime poems seek to bring order by becoming heedful of feminine energies and honoring them.

*   *   *

Shakespeare wrote only one play entirely in verse: Richard II. He clearly saw Richard II as a special case, describing the emergence of the modern out of the medieval in Henry IV's usurpation. The medieval world of hereditary rule, imaged by high-flown verse, was displaced by modern prose *real politick*, just as the Latin Mass was displaced by the Book of Common Prayer.

Also, Shakespeare, to show Richard a bad king, made of him a bad poet, his images flat, figures confused, eloquent words echoing hollow: not even angels could save him from the treasonous Bolingbroke. Other than this specialized instance, Shakespeare mixed prose and verse as appropriate to his characters and their subjects.

Eliot has a like sensitivity to poetic *register*. So long and ambitious a poem as Four Quartets would descend to monotone unless he varied the register. Moreover, certain subjects are not fit to discuss in lilting verse (as we will see especially at the beginning of The Dry Salvages). The poet must match his mode to his subject and, though critics complain, this method is correct.

20

*　　*　　*

In a sense, Eliot's Quartets, are Socratic. Plato's dialogues establish their premises, not by abstract argument, but by imitating conversation. As Wittgenstein said:

The correct method in philosophy would really be the following: to say nothing except what can be said, i.e. propositions of natural science – i.e. something that has nothing to do with philosophy – and then, whenever someone else wanted to say something metaphysical, to demonstrate to him that he had failed to give a meaning to certain signs in his propositions. Although it would not be satisfying to the other person – he would not have the feeling that we were teaching him philosophy – this method would be the only strictly correct one.[14]

The Socratic method is the paradigm of correct philosophy in that philosophy is, like medicine, remedial. The doctor who first infects his patient in order to cure him, does no good. Likewise, only the sophist offers false assertions in order to refute them.

*　　*　　*

In a sense, Four Quartets is an example of an ancient genre: the Confession. Confession, like the Gospel, is a literary genre made possible by Christianity and, like the Gospel, did not exist prior to Christianity. Confession describes the soul's journey to God, using the self as paradigm. As the story of a God-relationship is a love story, each person will have their own experience. That being said, happy relationships share things in common. These commonalities are the substance of Confession.

Of its nature, a Confession cannot begin happily: the soul must be lost before she gropes her way back to God. Dante's tale of St. Dominic (Paradiso 12), notwithstanding, no one is born a saint and even Christ learned obedience through suffering (Hebrews 5.8). This is doubly the case in the modern world "under conditions that seem unpropitious" (EC V.187-188).

*　　*　　*

21

Poetry differs from prose not only by rhyme and meter: it is not merely flowery prose. Prose transfers information, but Poetry makes us *feel*. The poet cannot tell us *what* to feel as we cannot be made to feel to order. The poet must, instead, offer a chain of images and situations evoking the desired emotion. The extent of the poet's success corresponds to the extent the reader feels the intended emotion. This theory has been (unfortunately) dubbed the "objective correlative."[15]

For the Four Quartets, as a whole, the objective correlative is Music. The poem "sings" in four contrasting "voices:"

1) The sensual voice (the heart) in images and formal devices.
2) The critical voice (the mind) in prosy philosophical reflection.
3) The meditative voice (the spirit) mediates the paradoxes of the two prior voices.
4) The Unitive voice (wisdom) is no voice to itself, but a choral performance of the three other voices.[16]

These "voices' give the poem its dialogic quality and the indirection necessary to poetic discourse.

*   *   *

As Eliot does not distinguish the various voices, we must recognize them by "ear." A reflective flatness marks the critical voice, providing a counterpoint to the spontaneity and overtly poetically devices of the sensual voice. They take turns in the first two movements, each illustrating the others' limitation. The first movements open with a contradiction (present in the past (BN), beginning as end (EC), river god-not god (DS) and midwinter spring (Little Gidding (LG))) to be clarified by a landscape meditation. The second movement begins with a lyric corresponding to the fourth movement. The lyrics act as prelude and postlude to the central "working" section of the poem. The second part of the second movement frames the question set by the prior contradiction and in the third movement the meditative voice takes on the ethical working out of a solution. In the fifth, the fourth voice, the unitive expression of the other three, states the solution to the initial problem, using poetic creation as analogy for the making of the soul.

*   *   *

Each poem approaches time and timelessness from a perspective embodied in an element of physical reality (BN (air), EC (earth), DS (water), LG (fire)). The modern poet cannot, like Dante, write about a man (who is every man), going on a paradigmatic journey. In the Middle Ages, one story so shaped a continent's imagination that one man's story *could* represent all, but as our modern age offers no canonical vision of what a human being is, Eliot emphasizes *exploration,* his counterpart to modern science's experimentation. Our voyage on the "great sea of being" (Paradiso 1.113) requires a compass. Modernity's vision is so limited and limiting that we need to augment it with some traditional practice that binds the world into a whole.

*   *   *

To be present is to be *here now*. Presence is not only temporal, but spatial as well. Each of the Quartets have as their correlative a place the poet revisits in memory. Without place, time is abstraction.

Time is a strange prison. We know no reason why we should be here rather than there and are often torn between where we are and where we would wish to be. We punish miscreants by shackling them, for a time, to a location to contemplate temporality in the form of walls and bars (Is penitentiary, perhaps, the modern monasticism?).

*   *   *

Eliot questions the relation of time and timelessness, the word and silence. How, he asks, can we be in time in a way that has eternal validity? How, he asks, can a poem, a sequence of words in time, mediate a timeless inward silence? His answer is the *pattern*. He cannot tell us how directly without falsifying his message by couching it in language, a time-bound medium. Hence, the need for an objective correlative, a series of images that do not explain, but *evoke* in the reader the right understanding free of the time-bound medium of words.

*   *   *

Eliot points out:

It is wrong to think that there are parts of the Divine Comedy which are of interest only to Catholics or to medievalists. For there is a difference (which here I hardly do more than assert) between philosophical <u>belief</u> and poetical <u>assent</u> . . . . In reading Dante you must enter the world of thirteenth century Catholicism: which is not the world of modern Catholicism, as his world of physics is not the world of modern physics. You are not called upon to believe what Dante believed, for your belief will not give you a groat's worth more of understanding and appreciation; but you are called upon more and more to understand it. If you can read poetry as poetry, you will "believe" in Dante's theology exactly as you believe in the physical reality of his journey; that is, you suspend both belief and disbelief.[17]*

Perhaps I can present this distinction more clearly by comparison. Thomas Aquinas' proofs for the existence of God were refuted because they rested on a "discarded image:"[18] falsify his premises and you refute his conclusion. His contemporary, Dante, shared the same premises, but falsifying his cosmology does him little harm. Why? He explained his Divine Comedy in a letter:

The subject, then, of the entire work, literally, is the state of souls after death, pure and simple. On that premise the whole work proceeds. But, understood allegorically, the work's subject is how the human, by his merits or demerits in the exercise of his free will, justly deserves reward or punishment. (Epistle XIII.24-25)

Thomas meant what he says about the cosmos to *describe* the cosmos, his arguments from cosmology bridges directly to his theology. As we no longer accept his cosmology, we lose his theology. But Dante's cosmology images a moral order: falsify his cosmological premises and you find he is talking about ethics. And, as it is ethically indifferent whether the sun revolves around the earth or the earth around the sun, we may fault him for a flawed analogy, but refuting his cosmology leaves his ethical claims intact.

*   *   *

The Four Quartets both is and is not a religious poem. It is religious in the sense of *religare* (Latin, the restoring of bonds): it attempts to restore the bond joining "God, man and world" to a unity. It is *not* religious in the sense of espousing a collection of doctrines about God's relation to humanity. Thus Eliot feels no compunction in alluding to Bhagavad Gita in one section of the poem (DS III) and Dante's Paradiso in the next (DS IV). He neither asserts the rightness nor wrongness of one set of doctrines in relation to the other; nor does he try to reconcile them. Instead, he claims that *prior to* the differentiation of various religious paths, there is a universal substratum called Word (logos) of which religions are concretions.

This logos is an object both of belief and disbelief. It is an object of belief in that, without prior belief in the logos, any subsequent religious belief is incoherent. It is an object of disbelief in that it is *empty*, the positive content of belief fully iinvested in religious doctrine. Deism is no religion, but a halfway house for those too cowardly for godlessness.

*   *   *

The Four Quartets is not a Christian poem. Eliot does not want to exclude anyone by the assertion of a specific religiosity. He is, in this, more generous than many of his critics whose goal is to exclude religiosity in general. It distresses them to see a religiosity they cannot ridicule as idiotic, bigoted, or simply out-moded thus "justifying" their scorn as a "public service."

The Box Circle

Burnt Norton

Burnt Norton relates oddly to the other poems: it is the only one among them originally published without a thought to its relation to the others. It, in fact, was intended as an only child. It appeared alone in Eliot's Collected Poems 1909-1935 as an epitaph, a more elegant and technically controlled version of The Waste Land: as The Waste Land cleansed of youthful excess. The plan of four poems each representing an element was conceived only after its publication. It could, luckily, be "shoe-horned" to fit by transposing its central image of light into the key of air.

* * *

Heraclitus' epigraph, in time shared in common by all the poems, was originally a single tenancy. This was in-keeping with Burnt Norton's relation to The Waste Land, which also had a Greek epigraph. When the other poems joined Burnt Norton, they followed its pursuit of a common understanding and thus could share the epigraph:
Although the Word is common to all, most men live as if by their own understanding.
Words are common and transactional, the means by which humans express their inward meanings outwardly in shared symbols. But words, the public means of transaction, are also the private means of thought. Here arises contradiction. As the Psalms say:
The fool says in his heart 'There is no God.' (Psalms 14.1, 53.1)
Why does the fool say it 'in his heart' (i.e. secretly)? Because he does not wish his neighbor hear him opting out of the common understanding to seek to profit at the neighbor's expense. His silence allows him to pass words of his own minting as the common coin.

* * *

When words fail to bind a people together, chaos ensues. Eliot, writing The Waste Land in the aftermath of World War I, lamented the loss of a common currency. Europe, tearing herself to pieces, had neither community nor communion. Nation perceived nation as competitor to be beaten, as prey to be hunted, or as carrion to pick over.

Such an age finds in Dante a useful diagnostic. His society had a sound currency and before we can assess our own situation we must know what that looked like. Dante assumed a prince, anointed by God, whose rule of law was the first step in his peoples' moral education (Purgatorio 16.94-96). In our age, the state either cedes its role as moral teacher, making each individual responsible for his or her own moral code or offers *itself* as an object of worship.

*   *   *

This makes it necessary, in our age, for the reader to take a share in constructing their world. Hence, the Four Quartets' elements do not cohere into a whole, but provide the ingredients necessary to form one. Hence the second epigraph:
The way up and the way down are the same.
A strange recipe! Eliot's central thesis is that in an age when the society at large has lost its moorings it becomes incumbent upon the individual to discover the Word for him or herself. Since modernity has stripped away the sense of the world, it cannot be regained by modern means: the individual must turn to traditional religious practice.

*   *   *

Eliot's division of the poem into five movements "camouflaged" the structure of its argument. That the way up and the way down are the same offers a clue to this hidden principle. The first and final movements are related as question and answer in a riddle. Immediately before and after are lyrics, the first is a division of the second movement, the second, a stand-alone fourth movement. Since these features, though

28

structurally analogous, are treated differently (one standing alone and the other subsumed into a larger structure) their functional likeness is not readily apparent. [19]

This hidden element is analogous to the world which cannot be taken at "face value." The Word is not immediately recognizable nor can it truthfully be represented as such. The Divine Comedy began with Dante's attempt to climb Mount Purgatory and wild beasts chasing him back to the dark forest. Once there, he meets Virgil who explains the way up is the way down: the path to Paradise leads through Hell.

The second half of the second movements and the third movements modulate from the premature attempt at ascension into descent. Only after a descent will vision descend on us.

Movement No. 1

Time present and time past
Are both perhaps present in time future
And time future contained in time past.
If all time is eternally present
All time is unredeemable.
What might have been is an abstraction
Remaining a perpetual possibility
Only in a world of speculation
What might have been and has been
Point to one end, which is always present. (I.1-10)

We begin with the critical voice droning on in a metaphysical mode. "Is time, perhaps, circular? Is the present in the past and both nested in the future?" he muses, offering his initial hypothesis cloaked in philosophical verbiage. Then he twists the knife, asking a further question (not stated as a question and couched in the negative): How is time to be redeemed?

*   *   *

29

What, if some day or night a demon were to steal after you into your loneliest loneliness and say to you: "This life as you now live it and have lived it, you will have to live once more and innumerable times more; and there will be nothing new in it, but every pain and every joy and every thought and everything unutterably small or great in your life will have to return to you, all in the same succession and sequence – even this spider in the moonlight between the trees, and even this moment and I myself. The eternal hourglass of existence is turned upside down again and again, and you with it, speck of dust!"[20]

Nietzsche, broaching his intuition, cannot speak it in his own voice (how would <u>he</u> know time's relation to eternity?). He, instead, attributes his idea to a demon, a being acquainted with eternity, who tempts him with "what if" much as Eliot does us with "perhaps . . . . if." And, like Eliot, Nietzsche claims a timeless moment inspired his ideas of eternal recurrence: in his case, a demon's discourse in a moonlit garden and, in Eliot's, a visionary moment in a sunlit garden.

*   *   *

I quoted, in the Preface to my book on Dante's Paradiso, Nietzsche misremembering the sign above the gates of Hell. I, focused on defending Dante, humorlessly missed a larger irony. Nietzsche, a man of much spirit but little wisdom, postulated the eternal recurrence of the same. He thus expressed his desire for eternity <u>and</u> his aversion to afterlives and other worlds. He believed that time, infinitely repeated in the future <u>and</u> the past would allow him to have eternity in <u>this</u> world. But ironically this idea replicated Dante's vision of Hell. There the damned eternally, obsessively repeat the sin that earned them damnation. Eliot seconds Dante's motion, pointing out that if Nietzsche is correct, time is Hell (unredeemable).

*   *   *

As Dante's pilgrim put it (questioning a damned soul):
"Ah, as I hope your seed shall soon find rest,"
    I asked, "help me untie that knot

30

That has here so tethered my thought.
It seems, if I hear right, that you can see,
  Beforehand, what time will bring us,
  But present things you see in a different way."
"We see, as those of imperfect sight,
  Those things" he said, "that are yet distant,
  So much light the Sovereign Lord allots,
But when events draw near, or are, our minds
  Are empty, and were none to bring us news
  We should know nothing of your human state." (Inferno
10.94-105)

The damned have a peculiar relation to time: they know past and future, but not the present. As we can repent *only* in the present, their punishment denies them that privilege. Their present is in the past, in the lives they lost, and they know the future as the outcome of a living present out of their sight.

*   *   *

Nietzsche confused the merely interminable with the eternal. Hell is not eternal (Inferno 3.7.-8), but began in time (Inferno 34.121-126). Hell <u>must</u> begin in time as Hell must be chosen before it can exist and choosing occurs only in time (choosing must cause a *change*, a time after that differs from the time before).[21] Nietzsche, as always, asked the right question even if his answer, as always, left something to be desired.

His answer, the eternal return of the same, is Hellish because when choice has a *necessary* outcome, freedom is abolished. Nietzsche, recognizing this consequence, welcomed it, exiling free will. If time, past, present and future, circle on a moebius strip, time is a closed system into which no newness enters. Time must have an *edge*.

*   *   *

I can guess about the past and what you mean about the future;
But a present is missing, needed to connect them.[22]

If free will is no abstraction, we are free only in the present. We cannot unwill the past, nor act on that not yet existing. Free will operates in the meantime between past and future. Consigning the present to the past collapses past and future (time before and time after) into each other. We choose here and now and see, as the *moment* of choosing recedes, what the tide leaves behind. We may choose our joy or regret, but we cannot know, in the *moment* of choosing, which we have chosen. Life must be lived forward, but understood, *backwards*.[23]

*   *   *

What might have been and what has been bracket our subject. What might have been never actually existed and can be imagined taking shape in any number of forms. What has been has irrevocably come to be in time and cannot have happened in any other way. Between the two lies immediacy, possible only in the present. Immediacy has been compared to a sleepwalker who awakes at the mention of his name,[24] for to think of the immediate is precisely to leave immediacy.

*   *   *

Footfalls echo in the memory
Down the passage we did not take
Towards the door we never opened
Into the rose garden. My words echo
Thus, in your mind.
            But to what purpose
Disturbing the dust on a bowl of rose-leaves
I do not know. (I.11-16)

We modulate from the critical to the sensual voice, no longer speaking of time past and future, but of footfalls, sounds indicative of motion in space. Footfalls echo, describing motion in "mental," not physical, space. Memories echo events. A dusty bowl of rose leaves recalls the afternoon in the rose garden. Then, the day was alive with possibility. Now we are left the desiccated remains. Why disturb their dust? To apologize for or

32

to justify their exhumation? The claim of ignorance arouses suspicions.

The garden path echoes with neglect, paths not taken and doors unopened. Perhaps these doors should remain shut. Perhaps we should not venture into the garden. But here we are, the air redolent of foreboding and regret.

*   *   *

The house in the Cotswalds was called Burnt Norton after an older house a suicidal owner burned down around himself. The manor, once housing a boys' school, is empty now, yet, off to the side, alive and flourishing, is a formal rose garden in the midst of which were dug two drained pools. The image transforms an emotional-psychological-spiritual state into landscape.

Eliot explored Burnt Norton's garden in 1934, with his American friend, Emily Hale. Eliot's marriage to Vivienne, from whom he had separated but would never divorce, was over. Eliot stayed married to her partly out of religious conviction, partly out of masochism, and partly to fend off Emily. She, in deluded dreams, saw Tom one day marrying her. We do not know the extent that Tom led her on (Eliot's letters to her will continue sealed until 2019, and we have reason to believe he destroyed hers to him[25]), but that she willingly followed. Vivienne died and (much later) to Emily's chagrin, Tom married a younger woman.

*   *   *

Five years earlier Eliot had written a long essay on Dante, going so far as to translate the garden scene where Dante and Beatrice are reunited (Purgatorio 30.31-48). He urged, if we wish to understand this scene, to read Dante's earlier work, Vita Nuova.[26] Dante, himself citing Vita Nuova in the passage, apparently agreed.

Dante set the scene for the reunion by gender confusion. Beatrice, invited to alight from her car, is referred to in the masculine gender (Purgatorio 30.19). Dante imagines Virgil as his Mamma (Purgatorio 30.44), tries to share a confidence with him, sister to sister (Purgatorio 30.46-48, Virgil, Aeneid 4.23) and, finding him gone, laments him as a beloved wife (Purgatorio 30.50-52, Virgil, Georgics 4.525-527). Beatrice, alighting from her carriage, is compared to an Admiral exhorting her sailors (Purgatorio 30.58-60). This prepares us for an exchange in which Beatrice will be the dominant (masculine) partner and Dante the submissive (feminine).

While Beatrice replaces Virgil as Dante's teacher, Eliot merely brings Emily along for the ride. She is not an individual but part of a "we." Dante is as engaged with Beatrice as Eliot is detached from Emily. Interpreting this as mere sexism on Eliot's part misses the point: despite a great loosening of sexual roles between Dante's and Eliot's eras, sexual reciprocity is more difficult in the modern age.*

*   *   *

Earlier cultures strove mightily to keep marriage free of love. Marriage was the legal means to transfer rights and honors, real estate and wealth from one generation to the next. It was necessarily a rational contract to maximize familial profit over generations. To this end, Eros, the irrational love that is unconcerned with profit and loss, had to be kept at bay.

The Greeks used pederasty (i.e. the love of boys) to draw erotic pursuit *away from* marriage. While married men slept with their wives in order to "renew the people," they were free to pursue, woo and, hopefully, win, the teen-aged boy of their choosing. Thus the Symposium's speeches on erotic love begin only *after* women are excluded. And that was the point, to keep erotic pursuit, an anti-social enterprise, away from marriage.

Likewise with the Courtly Love of the Middle Ages. Dante sired children with Gemma as per the agreement between

---

* Paradoxically, when modern programmers turned the Inferno into a computer game, they reversed the roles of the main characters making Beatrice the captive and Dante her rescuer.

their parents. The god of Love chose Beatrice as Dante's personal beloved. Gemma bore him Jacopo, Pietro and Antonia. Beatrice inspired Vita Nuova and the Divine Comedy. As Beatrice never slept in Dante's marriage bed, so Gemma never appeared in his poems (this is emphasized in Dante's protracted conversations with two cousins she grew up with (Purgatorio 23.42-24.93, Paradiso 3)). The point was to keep marriage and love separate.

*   *   *

Aristophanes, the comic poet, offered, in the fourth of the seven speeches of Symposium, a parable of the genesis of love. Originally, the earth was populated by the circle-people, the children of the Uranean gods. They had four arms, four legs and two sets of genitals. Some were of the Sun (male-male). Some were of the moon (female-female). And some were of the earth (male-female). The Olympian gods, feeling threatened, cast a sleep over them and surgically divided them in half, thereby creating the human race with individuals who feel, of themselves, incomplete and desire, through love, to find and rejoin their missing halves.

*   *   *

J. J. Rousseau invented the romantic novel in 1762 with his Emile. Immanuel Kant, on receiving his copy, hunkered down so engrossed he missed the afternoon walk by which his neighbors set their clocks. They called the police fearing foul play. Such was Rousseau's power. And it was amplified when his heirs in music (Beethoven), letters (Goethe) and philosophy (Kant) took over the culture.

*   *   *

In the union of the sexes each contributes to the common aim, but not in the same way. From this diversity arises the first assignable difference in the moral relations of the two sexes. One ought to be active

35

and strong, the other passive and weak. One must necessarily will and be able; it suffices the other put up little resistance.

Once the principle is established, it follows that woman is made specially to please man. If man ought to please her, it is due to a less direct necessity. His merit is his power; he pleases by the sole fact of his strength. This is not the law of love, I agree. But it is that of nature, prior to love itself.[27]

Rousseau's romantic model is complementary, each partner contributing to the other's completion by performing differing tasks. There is also a junior and a senior partner. The woman attracts the man by charm and beauty, the man brings the woman and her children under his protection and she, in return, is subject to him. If this sounds like hostage taking, Rousseau agrees: it is not the law of love, but that of *nature*.

*   *   *

If we blame the Bible for the romantic model's exclusive heterosexuality, it remains blameless for its most deleterious feature: the mixing of love and marriage. Instead of using erotic pursuit as "safety valve," ancillary to marriage, marriage begins in erotic intoxication, in two people choosing each other, without regard to utility, to bind themselves to each other in a lifelong contract. But while marriage is a lifelong commitment, the erotic intoxication that occasioned it has a shelf life. Sooner rather than later, we awake with a hangover to discover the woman we married is not the girl we chased. The girl was a projection of our own emotional need. The woman is an independent creature with her own emotional history. We must decided whether we are willing, stone cold sober, to pay the freight for this unasked for burden.

The operative phrase is "stone cold sober." A man, in the throes of erotic intoxication, will say *anything and mean it* if he gets the girl, as he fears not getting the girl, will bring about the apocalypse. Earlier cultures kept the choice of partner out of the hands of the lovers because the mind and will are not on speaking terms. Or, more truthfully, the will does not speak in words. If I can explain in words why I love someone, I am lying.

This is why Hallmark is in business as the impersonal surrogate of lovers everywhere. The springs of love are an unspeakable mystery and how can we lay the basis of a foundational institution of society on a mystery?

*   *   *

Later, Eliot will admit:
We had the experience but missed the meaning,
And approach to the meaning restores the experience
In a different form, beyond any meaning
We can assign to happiness. (DS II.93-96)
Eliot was a poet, but no lover. He did all in his power to subvert romanticism in his verse, but was helpless in his love. We, standing near the end of the process he began in his poems, are better placed to understand its implications. Dante, being no romantic, had no need to subsume Beatrice to himself as Eliot did Emily. Beatrice, as Dante's muse, was unattainable. But Eliot's romanticism consisted in the confusion of erotically pursuing his muse. But the muse is unattainable because she is a projection of his own poetic powers. The confusion is not simply Eliot's but that of an entire culture.

*   *   *

The vision of woman bearing flowers out of sunlight goes back to The Waste Land:
"You gave me Hyacinths a year ago;
"They called me the hyacinth girl."
Yet when we came back, late, from the Hyacinth garden,
Your arms full, and your hair wet, I could not
Speak and my eyes failed, I was neither
Living nor dead, and I knew nothing,
Looking into the heart of light. (Waste Land I.35-41)
The young poet saw in the Hyacinth girl (the gift of natural love between man and woman) an image of despair. He cannot accept the offered flowers, he cannot speak and his eyes fail. Like

Dante, looking on Satan, he is neither alive nor dead (Inferno 34.22-27).

Emily, in middle age, offered Eliot a second chance at love, but though he still cannot accept, this time he achieves a new vision: not of natural love healing his heart, but a religious love making him happy without bringing an earthly happiness. The old man's vision differs from the young man's by the ministry of Virgil (Vivienne[28]) who, leading him through Hell and Purgatory, opens a new wisdom.

*   *   *

Other echoes
Inhabit the garden. Shall we follow?
Quick said the bird, find them, find them,
Round the corner. Through the first gate,
Into our first world, shall we follow
The deception of the thrush? Into our first world.
There they were, dignified, invisible,
Moving without pressure, over the dead leaves,
In the autumn heat, through the vibrant air, (I.17-25)

We are not alone in the garden. Who are these "other echoes" sharing it?[29] Four Quartets is a haunted poem. Each Quartet has its ghosts (except for Dry Salvages, where we find "dead foreign men" (DS I.23), "dead negroes" (DS II.116) and a prayer to Our Lady for widows and mothers who have lost husbands or sons (DS IV.180-181)). The ghosts are bygone images: Medieval Elyots twirling, arm in arm, around a fire (EC I.23-46) and the compound ghost of poetic tradition coaching Eliot on what to expect from his future (LG II.78-149). The absence of ghosts in The Dry Salvages may well refer to the past the popular mind wishes to disown (DS II.89). Are the ghosts in this garden Adam and Eve as this is our first world? The Miltonian language describing "them" might lead to that interpretation.[30] While they may be seen in a number of ways (Adam and Eve, parents, the youthful Emily and Eliot) their "pastness" is their essential quality.

And the bird called, in response to
The unheard music hidden in the shrubbery,
And the unseen eyebeam crossed, for the roses
Had the look of flowers that are looked at.
There they were as our guests, accepted and accepting.
So we moved, and they, in a formal pattern, (I.26-31)

And what about this talking, deceiving animal (the thrush), does he replace a serpent?[31] Certainly, he is the new source of conflict. Air, as element, represents thought. Thought, mediated by language, unfolds in time. The mind flashes simultaneously, opening out in an instant of vision. Words draw eternal visions into the web of an alien medium, time. Language coins vision into thought, word following word building into signification. Words express vision as money signifies value.

Eliot's guide, in this airy poem, is a bird who, flying, negotiates the element of air as the poet negotiates language. But there are guides and guides. The bird leads us into the garden and tells us to leave, but is useless while we are there, and, in fact, as we leave, steals from us what we might have gained from our visit.[32]

*   *   *

We move through the rose garden and they move with us in formal pattern. We waltz to unheard music. Neither the rustle of dry leaves dents our ears, nor the vision of roses disturbs our sight. The image, the poet reminds us, is not sensual. Memory is a remove from the actual.

But none of this is my memory. I, though with them, was unborn in 1934. I scan a page many years later, trying to understand what the poet meant as he scribbled and crossed out, paced and swore, musing on how to choreograph words to his dance. He echoes thus in my mind.

*   *   *

Along the empty alley, into the box circle,
To look down into the drained pool.
Dry the pool, dry concrete, brown edged,
And the pool was filled with water out of sunlight,
And the lotos rose, quietly, quietly,
The surface glittered out of heart of light,
And they were behind us, reflected in the pool.
Then a cloud passed, and the pool was empty. (I.32-39)

At the center of the garden-world are two pools, one semi-circular, one rectangular: the box circle, representing two religious paths. Then is the epiphany and language fails, for to say the pools filled with water implies that it did so in time, but one moment they were empty, then they were full, and then empty again without passing through an intermediate state. The poet describes an "event" that did not happen in time. Thus the water came 'out of sunlight' and disappeared with a passing cloud.

The religious love, the love of no particular thing, is pictured in a double flowering. The lotus, Lord Krishna's throne, arose from the murky pool in luminous beauty. The lotus is the second birth. The rose, both verb and noun, is, in Paradiso, the ever-opening arena where the saints share the vision of God.

And he sees, reflected in the water, images of the other echoes with whom they have shared the garden. How are these images reflected in a medium? Do they vanish with their reflections when the medium vanishes?

*   *   *

Go, said the bird, for the leaves were full of children,
Hidden excitedly, containing laughter.
Go, go, go, said the bird: human kind
Cannot bear very much reality. (I.40-43)

This is no time for foolish questions. The bird, who had invited them into the garden, now urgently bids them go, repeating words ("Human kind cannot bear very much reality.") Eliot had placed in the mouth of Thomas Becket before his martyrdom.[33] Archbishop Thomas said goodbye to his Priests, prophesying a sword will pierce their hearts with a grief that is joy (Luke 2:35) when they understand, in retrospect, what had taken place. Their memories will be intermittent: forgetting as they work, remembering by the fire. And each "remembering" will subtly differ from any before: a new experience at a greater remove from the past event. With this, the bird casts us out of the garden. And the ghosts of the children who might have been, have all they can do not to laugh at us, for they live, world without end, in the garden.

*   *   *

Time past and time future
What might have been and what has been
Point to one end, which is always present (Lines I.44-46)

And, at the coda, the critical voice returns us to the home key. This time, however, he qualifies less ("perhaps" or "if" are gone). He is not musing but making a statement: Time future and past point to a single moment: the present moment.

Movement No. 2

Garlic and sapphires in the mud
Clot the bedded axle-tree.
The thrilling wire in the blood
Sings below inveterate scars
Appeasing long forgotten wars.
The dance along the artery
The circulation of the lymph
Are figured in the drift of stars (II.47-54)

Near the house, a tree overlooks the garden. Eliot observed the play of the light on its figured leaves.[34] The tree, transfigured, is the World Ash tree of Norse mythology. This symbol of the universe, reduced to its base elements, is plant and mineral clotted together by the blood of animals. The tree is axled to enable its turning with the seasons of birth and of death, war and peace. Wars, long over, still thrill the rivers of our blood, the land pockmarked by a punishing history. The cycle of blood through the body figures the courses of stars through the heavens. Macrocosm and microcosm coalesce.

*   *   *

Heraclitus saw the world as a synthesis of opposites. Opposite elements (garlic and sapphires) in their strife, make the world. The world is in flux, with one element and then its opposite gaining ascendancy. Thus, paradoxically, things maintain their identities, not by staying what they are, but by constantly becoming what they were not. The world is not a body, it is a Word (logos).

This Word is no flatus vocis, no puff of air, dispersing into nothing. The Word, to be word, must bear a meaning. John, in his gospel, distinguishes Word from noise when Jesus says:
Why do you not understand what I say (lalia)?
It is because you cannot bear to hear my word (logos). (John 8.43)
The word without meaning (lalia) is as dead as flesh without breath. Meaning gives the Word life. This meaning comes of discerning the *pattern*.

*   *   *

Ascend to summer in the tree
We move above the moving tree
In light upon the figured leaf
And hear upon the sodden floor
Below, the boarhound and the boar
Pursue their pattern as before
But reconciled among the stars. (II.55-60)
We begin our ascent in a dream. We soar above the tree and, like Dante in the eighth Heaven (Paradiso 22.133-153, 27.79-87), look back at the threshing floor of the earth. Distant sounds of conflict arise from below, but we can ignore them, assuming that those earth makes enemies are friends among the stars.[35]

*   *   *

Such a consciousness is dreaming. How would the world appear to an awakened one? Buddha awoke sitting beneath the Bodhi tree. He awakened to the four noble truths:

1)   The Buddha awoke to a world in flux. Birth is suffering, decay is suffering, death is suffering. Union with the unpleasant is suffering as is separation from the pleasing. "Happiness" derived from possessing that you <u>must</u> one day lose, teaches you, on the day of loss, that your "happiness" was actually suffering. Suffering rests on the delusion that we can keep the object of our desires when all objects <u>must</u> be surrendered.

2)   The Buddha awoke to see that suffering derives from desire, the desire for pleasures, for dominance over others or for riches. We, failing to recognize the necessity of change, reach in desire for objects or experiences. But no object or experience can gladden us durably as every object or experience <u>must</u> be surrendered.

3)   The Buddha awoke to see that suffering ends with the cessation of desiring. Spiritual practice should aim at the cessation of suffering (Nirvana). Suffering ceases when we no longer seek happiness in objects or experiences that <u>must</u> be surrendered.

4)   The Buddha awoke to see the path to the end of desire is eight-fold:

    a) Right View: understanding the world as a flux. We keep nothing we have.

    b) Right Intention: knowing right from wrong and doing right to the exclusion of the wrong.

    c) Right Speech: abstaining from lies, abuse, gossip and idle chatter.

    d) Right Action: abstaining from theft, murder and illicit sex.

    e) Right Livelihood: abstaining from dishonesty in business and from professions causing others harm.

f) Right Effort: doing and thinking those things leading to enlightenment and avoiding those things that merely dull the senses.

g) Right Mindfulness: the continual awareness of body and mind that one may not transgress due to inattention.

h) Right Concentration: meditation to focus the mind and enable detachment from emotional and mental states. [36]

The eight-fold path is pictured as a wheel because it is not a series of steps to be completed in sequence, but mutually reinforcing disciplines to be developed simultaneously. The cultivation of one discipline aids the cultivation of all the others.

*   *   *

At the still point of the turning world. Neither flesh nor fleshless;
Neither from nor towards; at the still point, there the dance is,
But neither arrest nor movement. And do not call it fixity,
Where past and future are gathered. Neither movement from nor towards,
Neither ascent nor decline. Except for the point, the still point,
There would be no dance, and there is only the dance.
I can only say, there we have been: but I cannot say where.
And I cannot say, how long, for that is to place it in time. (II.62-69)

The critical voice describes what enlightenment is *not*. Rotation is motion restricted to a point in space. Without the point, there is no motion but it is not, itself, in motion. Rotation is neither motion from nor toward, neither advance nor retreat. I cannot place the point in space without placing it in time. Nor can I place it in time without finding it in space. To locate it is to destroy it (just as the *present* cannot be located in the future or the past without destroying both future and past).

As the wheel revolves around the unmoving hub; so, as we cease to turn with the turning world it revolves around us, leaving us still. When the wheel of the world becomes the wheel of Dharma, our practice transforms our world.

44

The inner freedom from the practical desire,
The release from action and suffering, release from the inner
And the outer compulsion, yet surrounded
By a grace of sense, a white light still and moving,
Erhebung without motion, concentration
Without elimination, both a new world
And the old made explicit, understood
In the completion of its partial ecstasy,
The resolution of its partial horror.
Yet the enchainment of past and future
Woven in the weakness of the changing body,
Protects mankind from heaven and damnation
Which flesh cannot endure. (II.70-82)

Eliot moves from negation to affirmation. Nirvana is freedom from want, as we desire nothing. It is escape from the search for pleasure and the flight from pain. It is release from the fear of death. It is grace in the exaltation of enlightenment. It is coming into harmony with the world by no longer striving to master or own or enjoy it, but simply letting it *be*. It is to become human, to accept being human, living in the world realistically.

Yet desire is "woven into the weakness of the changing body." It is not easy to extirpate desire, for desire begins, not as vice, but as hunger. Life must compromise with desire, though the compromise is inherently dangerous. The body desires not only what sustains life, but what, taken in excess, brings pleasure. And pleasure needs no advocate as it is its own argument.

*   *   *

Time past and time future
Allow but a little consciousness.
To be conscious is not to be in time
But only in time can the moment in the rose-garden,
The moment in the arbour where the rain beat,
The moment in the draughty church at smokefall

Be remembered; involved with past and future.
Only through time time is conquered. (II.82-89)

Kant claimed that time and space are not things "out there." We cannot know what is "out there," but only the images our senses bring us. But the senses require time to order our experience (if everything happened at once, our overloaded senses would perceive nothing). Our senses, moreover, require space (if everything happened in the same place, we would, again, perceive only the overload). Time and space are not "out there," but are prerequisites for our knowing anything about "out there." Kant stoutly affirmed the existence of "out there," but as stoutly denied that we can know anything about it. This position is called "Kantian skepticism."

This is the enchainment of past and future. Time and space must somehow exist, but we cannot know how because we can only know the world as mediated by our senses which limit our perceptions as our minds arrange them in time and space. If time and space are fictions necessary to our continued being in the world, *we* will never know about it. The world is a dream from which we cannot wake.

*   *   *

Time past and time future so plague us with hopes and regrets that we can be little present in the *moment*. To be in the *moment* is not to be in time, but at the still point. To be in the *moment* is to be totally absorbed. There is no time to take in the *moment*, to feel its significance.

We can only, in some after-time, reflect on the *moment* of experience. But here lies danger. As the Buddhists say: "If you meet the Buddha on the road, kill him," that is, if you have some wonderful spiritual experience, don't forget to spoil it: otherwise you will be tempted to try and relive it.

Movement No. 3

We have been here before. In The Waste Land Eliot
wrote:
Unreal City,
Under the brown fog of winter dawn,
A crowd flowed over London Bridge, so many,
I had not thought death had undone so many. (Waste Land I.60-63)
Alluding to:
Behind that banner trailed so long a file
> *Of people – that I should have never believed*
> *That death had undone so many. (Inferno 3.55-57)*

Dante, awaiting the ferry into Hell, asked Virgil why
everyone was in such a hurry: they are on their way to eternal
damnation. Virgil answered Divine justice decreed that as, in
life, they perversely rushed to commit the sins that earned them
damnation, they should rush as eagerly to their punishment.
Here we are again presented with the rush hour – to work.

*   *   *

Here is a place of disaffection
Time before and time after
In a dim light: neither daylight
Investing form with lucid stillness
Turning shadow into transient beauty
With slow rotation suggesting permanence
Nor darkness to purify the soul
Emptying the sensual with deprivation
Cleansing affection from the temporal.
Neither plenitude nor vacancy. (III.90-99)

In the previous movement Eliot rose above the fray. In
this, he descends to the underworld. Eliot, living above a tube
station, took the subway to work and in that underworld, he
reflects on time before and time after.

*   *   *

He reflects on the quality of the light or its lack. It is here
only for its *utility*, to keep us from bumping into things as we

find our seats or to allow us to read the paper on the way into town. He reflects on its *artificiality*, it is not the true illumination of the sun, but a stand-in adequate to a limited purpose. Neither plenitude nor vacancy, it is something in between. Mediocrity is endemic to modernity, where the general run of humankind rule and any pretense to taste is elitism, a crime against nature. The light in the subway is good enough to see by just as the air is good enough to breathe. Who am I to say otherwise?

*   *   *

The true light, the sun, radiates in all directions and, its track across the sky is the source of time, but we moderns, so used to artificial light, forget our watches once imaged the heavens, and, for convenient reading, turn them into digital counters of abstract units.

Our cities, lit 24/7 with artificial light, banish the stars, the light of heaven. It has been supposed that human culture stems from our upright posture as we are the only animal who can contemplate the stars. Now artificial light allows us, at all times, to contemplate the work of human hands while blotting out the transcendent.

*   *   *

Only a flicker
Over the strained time-ridden faces
Distracted from distraction by distraction
Filled with fancies and empty of meaning
Tumid apathy with no concentration
Men and bits of paper, whirled by the cold wind
That blows before and after time,
Wind in and out of unwholesome lungs
Time before and time after.
Eructation of unhealthy souls
Into the faded air, the torpid
Driven on the wind that sweeps the gloomy hills of London,
Hampstead and Clerkenwell, Campden and Putney,

48

Highgate, Primrose and Ludgate. Not here
Not here the darkness, in this twittering world. (III.99-113)

Eliot moves from the light to what it discloses: the faces of a people disconnected from being. They, like the lights, are not fully dead, but alive enough only to be of use. They live to commute and commute to consume, distracting themselves from the distraction of their work with the distraction of their play. They dream of what they will buy to make themselves happy when nothing you can buy can make you happy.

Modernity hates extremes – blessing only those who shop until they drop. When all rank is leveled, things are all that people can agree on. The only distinctions are between brands, BMW versus Mercedes. Life loses meaning when conceived in terms of what we *use* and not what we *serve*.

*   *   *

As the Greeks had a single word ('pharmakon') for our words 'poison' and 'medicine' (dosage determining the difference), so they had one word ('pneuma') for our words 'breath' and 'wind.' Breath, the animating principle, distinguishes a living person from a corpse. The wind, an external force, sets lifeless things in motion. Here, the air, in "unwholesome lungs," is coughed out as something less than breath. Here, the subway is wind, driving commuters, like bits of paper, to their work places.

*   *   *

Descend lower, descend only
Into the world of perpetual solitude,
World not world, but that which is not world,
Internal darkness, deprivation
And destitution of all property,
Desiccation of the world of sense,
Evacuation of the world of fancy,
Inoperancy of the world of spirit;
This is the one way, and the other

49

Is the same, not in movement
But abstention from movement; while the world moves
In appetency, on its metalled ways
Of time past and time future. (III.115-127)

It may seem odd to use negative terms like "inoperancy," "destitution" "deprivation," when speaking of spirituality, but the spiritual life begins only after the surrender of positive terms. Ambition precludes spirituality. The first terrace of Dante's Purgatory banishes pride. This is necessary, otherwise pride would pervert spiritual exercises into competitions.

If we can plan to reach our goal, our goal is not spiritual. If we can chart a path to our goal, our goal is not spiritual. If we can bring our goal within reach, our goal is not spiritual. Spirituality is not a goal to be attained, but a striving for that we can neither deserve nor compass. To do what can be done, what we have power to do demands nothing of us. Faith demands the impossible.

*   *   *

There is striving and striving. The Sopranos, a fascinating TV series, was ostensively a crime drama, but actually centered on a therapeutic relationship. The series began when Dr. Melfi chose to treat mafia boss, Tony Soprano's, depression. It ended with her final clarity that Prozac and talking cures only helped him defray the emotional and spiritual cost of his nefarious enterprises, making him a better adjusted and more efficient psychopath.

Ethics and Medicine are two different things. In one episode Melfi was raped and the rapist escaped punishment on a technicality. All she had to do was tell Tony and he would have avenged her, but she could not allow Tony to commit a crime *for her*. She could see, in her personal life, that that would be wrong. But, to stop enabling Tony's criminal career, she had to read that treating people like him was *ineffective* (not wrong).

Melfi's medical training precluded her recognizing Tony's depression as a healthful response to his life of crime, his conscience screaming at him, "Stop, Thief." In her value-neutral medical judgment," depression is, in all cases, a disorder to be treated. So she treated him seven years before realizing she should not have treated him at all, that his only health lay in the disease (EC IV.152).

*   *   *

Modern medicine has colonized psychology. Under a medical model, all psychological states are reducible to physical states. Medical psychology is value-neutral because every ailment is a physical disorder to be remedied by a pill, a shot or a capsule. The soul is simply something about the body, and we are no more morally responsible for our spiritual state than for the color of our eyes.

But traditional psychology recognizes conditions ("the dark night of the soul," "the gift of tears") where prolonged, profound depression heralds the near approach of God. God is Light and Its approach discloses much we would keep hidden. Even from ourselves. Thus, God's approach is painful.

Movement No. 4

Time and the bell have buried the day,
The black cloud carries the sun away.
Will the sunflower turn to us, will the clematis
Stray down, bend to us; tendril and spray
Clutch and cling?
Chill
Fingers of yew be curled
Down on us? After the kingfisher's wing
Has answered light to light, and is silent, the light is still
At the still point of the turning world. (IV.127-136)

Burnt Norton's descending lyric poses a single question: as the black cloud of death envelopes the sun of life, will the sunflower turn to us? Will a vine reach into the earth for our resurrection?

*   *   *

Mrs. Perkins, Emily Hale's aunt, was an accomplished gardener, tending to vines and flowers. Eliot visited the Perkins to see Emily, and, in thanks, wrote lines 129-131 to his hostess, recalling the beauty of her garden.[37] Here he turns that preexisting lyric into a question about the afterlife.

*   *   *

The "chill fingers of yew" call to mind my childhood favorite Shakespeare song:
Come away, come away death,
And in sad cypress let me be laid.
Fly away, fly away, breath;
I am slain by a fair cruel maid.
My shroud of white, stuck all with yew,
O prepare it!
My part of death, no one so true
Did share it, (Twelfth Night II.4)
The lover, undone by unrequited love, wishes none to mourn him dead, as his beloved will not. As his shroud, "stuck all with yew," is prepared, so "chill fingers of yew" threaten to curl down on us, leaving our corpse cold, alone, unloved, bereft.

*   *   *

In the fall of 1933, Eliot paid a number of visits to the headquarters of the Society of Sacred Mission in Kelham, an Anglican religious community devoted to theological education. One day, near the Church yard, Eliot came across a kingfisher. The Church yard had a yew tree and masses of clematis. The two students who were with him that day, said he was very excited.[38]

*   *   *

He alludes also to Gerard Manley Hopkins:
As kingfishers catch fire, dragonflies dráw fláme;

52

As tumbled over rim in roundy wells
Stones ring; like each tucked string tells, each hung bell's Bow swung
finds tongue to fling out broad its name;
Each mortal thing does one thing and the same:
Deals out that being indoors each one dwells;
Selves — goes itself; myself it speaks and spells,
Crying Whát I do is me: for that I came.
Í say móre: the just man justices;
Kéeps gráce: thát keeps all his goings graces;
Acts in God's eye what in God's eye he is —
Chríst — for Christ plays in ten thousand places,
Lovely in limbs, and lovely in eyes not his
To the Father through the features of men's faces.

Hopkins begins with five images: two visual and three aural. Kingfishers and dragonflies, wings struck by the light, mirror it back, bright as fire. Stones, falling into wells, splash; stringed instruments, plucked, sing and bells, struck, ring. Thus each expresses its nature (speaking outwardly what lies "indoors"). So doing, each proclaims, "What I do is me: for that I came." The kingfisher need not speak his answer (unlike the thrush in the garden): his wing, reflecting the light of God, speaks his inner meaning. As animals and inanimate objects outwardly express their inward nature in their various operations, so moral man, by his living, expresses Christ alive in him. Considering the self as *larva dei,* a mask of God, we begin to transcend the loneliness of modernity which, by attempting to place all things in space and time, destroys every holy joy.

Movement No. 5

Words move, music moves
Only in time; but that which is only living
Can only die. Words, after speech, reach
Into the silence. Only by the form, the pattern,
Can words or music reach
The stillness, as a Chinese jar still
Moves perpetually in its stillness.(V.137-143)

The words "reaching" into silence are not those currently hanging in the air. Such words, only living, can only die. Words, after speech, echo in our minds, reverberate in a timeless inner silence. Wittgenstein said, "that of which we cannot speak, we should pass over in silence,"[39] but took it back. That we cannot speak of is too important to leave in silence as it is the unspeakable mystery of being: that there is anything and not nothing (what he called the "mystical"[40]). This mystery is literally unspeakable, for, when I speak of what is actual, meaning recedes from my words revealing them as only a token.

*   *   *

Heard melodies are sweet, but those unheard
Are sweeter; therefore, ye soft pipes, play on;
Not to the sensual ear, but, more endear'd,
Pipe to the spirit ditties of no tone:
Fair youth, beneath the trees, thou canst not leave
Thy song, nor ever can those trees be bare;
Bold Lover, never, never canst thou kiss,
Though winning near the goal yet, do not grieve;
She cannot fade, though thou hast not thy bliss,
For ever wilt thou love, and she be fair! (Keats, Ode to a Grecian Urn)
Keats praises the stillness of a Grecian Urn (the source of Eliot's "Chinese jar")[41], on which the image of a musician plays silent pipes, trees never shed their leaves, a young lover never kisses his beloved and a girl's beauty never fades. The static image fires the poet's imagination, evoking in him a desire for beauty as timeless as truth.

A word is never what it represents any more than a mirror's image is that reflected. The pattern of words cannot, themselves, be silent, but they can evoke silence in the reader. If the pattern of words reminds the reader to be present to silence, then it can, without contradiction, speak to silence.

*   *   *

Not the stillness of the violin, while the note lasts,

Not that only, but the co-existence,
Or say that the end precedes the beginning,
And the end and the beginning were always there
Before the beginning and after the end.
And all is always now. (V.144-149)

Eliot speaks of words and music as images of a deeper truth. We speak of music evoking silence, but not only that. We speak also of co-existence. What, in turning, has its end before its beginning and its beginning before it end? A Wheel.

A wheel is a co-existence. In turning it imitates the eternal stars. In turning it moves through time and space (Genesis 1.14). We are always at the crossroads of time before and time after, the still point of the turning world. That crossroad is, even when we are still and the world turns around us, ever in motion, the present ever rushing into the past. Thus it is always now and now always in motion.

*   *   *

Words strain,
Crack and sometimes break, under the burden,
Under the tension, slip, slide, perish,
Decay with imprecision, will not stay in place,
Will not stay still. Shrieking voices
Scolding, mocking, or merely chattering,
Always assail them. The Word in the desert
Is most attacked by voices of temptation,
The crying shadow in the funeral dance,
The loud lament of the disconsolate chimera. (V.149-158)

Eliot delivers an example of what he means: the word, here, a double-entendre, a co-existence. It is both the word, the device by which human being communicate with each other and the form of all things that have come into existence. As poet, Eliot deals in both and the two are co-existent. By words he evokes the Word much as Dante had done centuries before. But Eliot cannot replicate Dante (even if he had the skill). Modern times present the poet new challenges. Dante's solution cannot withstand the assault of modern solipsism. How can Dante answer the division of the world into the physical and the mental when he did not believe in a physical world?

*   *   *

Dante, like all ancient and medieval people, believed in the Word. Whether they were pagans like Heraclitus (agnostic whether God took interest in the world) or Christians like Dante (passionately convinced that It did) they believed that Word was the "stuff" of the world, that the world was an *idea,* hence its rationality. Thus the world was a cosmos, an order.

The modern problem is the Cartesian split between mind and matter, subject and object. Ancient and Medieval people did not split off their sense perception from the objects perceived. They believed that the sun rose in the east and set in the west because that was what it looked like. We moderns, through our use of complex mathematics and fantastically powerful instruments of measurement, have come to know more about the world at the price of being at home in it, making ourselves strangers in it; our aims and goals at variance with the planet's.

*   *   *

The Word, wandering the wilderness of Cartesian doubt, is tempted from all sides. Eliot mentions two:
1) Those who despairingly see death as extinction feel themselves a cosmic mistake. No animal who will die should know of it in advance.[42]
2) The chimera is a beast who, partaking the nature of two other beasts, is actually neither. These are anesthetized by dreams of neither plenitude nor vacancy.

*   *   *

While the Buddha described Dharma as a wheel, Christians prefer the image of a ladder describing the path to perfection unfolding in time:

56

The detail of the pattern is movement,
As in the figure of the ten stairs.
Desire itself is movement
Not in itself desirable;
Love is itself unmoving,
Only the cause and end of movement,
Timeless, and undesiring
Except in the aspect of time
Caught in the form of limitation
Between un-being and being.
Sudden in a shaft of sunlight
Even while the dust moves
There rises the hidden laughter
Of children in the foliage
Quick now, here, now, always —
Ridiculous the waste sad time
Stretching before and after. (V. 159-175)

The movement Eliot describes as the "detail of the pattern" is climbing and the ten stairs are from John of the Cross:

1)   The soul, sick with love, loses her taste for earthly things, desiring only the Beloved.
2)   The soul rises ceaselessly seeking her Beloved.
3)   The soul works tirelessly for the Beloved, as Jacob who, having worked seven years for Rachel, but given Leah, worked seven years more to have his beloved (Genesis 29.20)
4)   The soul suffers tirelessly for the Beloved, taking pleasure only in the Beloved's happiness.
5)   The soul grows impatient, imagining, at every moment, the Beloved in her grasp, and, at every moment, frustrated.
6)   The soul runs swiftly to the Beloved, touching Him repeatedly. She mounts up on wings like an eagle; she runs and does not weary.
7)   The Beloved makes the soul bold to approach Him.
8)   The Beloved takes the soul to Himself and unites with her. Mystical union.
9)   The soul alight, flaming with the glory of the Beloved. A temporary beatific vision in the body.

10) The soul becomes wholly assimilated into the Beloved. Heavenly beatitude.

*   *   *

The Beloved is Love itself, the uncaused cause of motion. In Dante's cosmology, the ninth and swiftest Heaven, the Primo Mobile, turns as God, in the Tenth Heaven, is still. It turns erotically drawn by her desire for completion: the desire for God. The Primo Mobile is the boundary between time, space and timeless Being, ever-spinning, bold with desire.

Desire is not of itself desirable because desire requires an *object*. Desire is not itself desirable, as desire is desire *for* something. Moreover, as it is redundant to desire that we already possess, we can only desire that we do not have. Thus the first step up St. John's ladder requires the soul to lose her taste for earthly objects and turn herself to God.

*   *   *

Dante, in the Heaven of Mars, compares the Blessed Souls to dust motes seen through a missing slat in a blind (Paradiso 14.109-117), moving in different directions and at various speeds, but all illumined by a single ray of light. Even in time and limitation, we hear the laughing voices of children, unborn and yet present. And the bird speaks in benediction, though we are no longer in the garden.

*   *   *

Whether we imagine enlightenment synergistically as a wheel, or sequentially as a ladder matters little as both movements begin in an initial turning. The Buddhist begins by recognizing that living in the world of the senses is like dwelling in a burning house: it is foolish to make yourself comfortable in a place from which you should escape. Likewise, the first step on St. John's ladder is a nausea with the world of the senses and a desire for the transcendent.

58

Desire is always desire *for* something: the value of desire determined by its *object*. Desire for a vulgar object is vulgar. Desire for a noble object is noble. The desire for temporal goods is vulgar; only the desire for eternity is noble. Even the pagans were clear about this (Plato, Symposium 206a), that this notion requires defending is the hallmark of a decedent (i.e. Post-Christian) age.

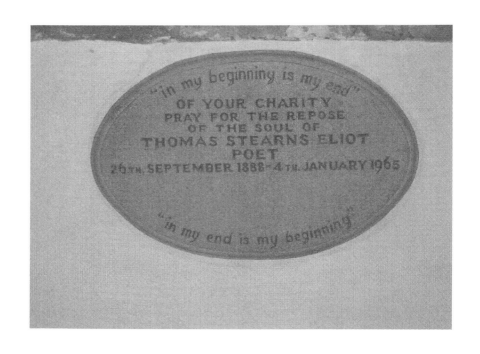

Eliot's Memorial

East Coker

Burnt Norton might have remained by itself if it hadn't been for the war, because I had become very much absorbed in the problems of writing for the stage and might have gone straight from The Family Reunion to another play. The war destroyed that interest for a time: you remember how the conditions of our lives changed, how much we were thrown on to ourselves in the early days? East Coker was the result – and it was only in writing East Coker that I began to see the Quartets as a set of four. [43]

Eliot's move from poetry to theatre was a change of focus. He had lost interest in poetry as the expression of a personal feeling, ready to assume the role of public poet (i.e. "the educator of the people" (Plato, Republic 10.606e)). The transition was initially successful. Murder in the Cathedral, his first play, saw two professional revivals in his lifetime and became a staple among amateur players. But his next play, The Family Reunion, closed after only five weeks on the West End. Then the war closed the theatres.

If Burnt Norton was meant to complete the circle of his poetry, the new war made The Waste Land's post-war lament seem a young man's grouse against the world. As the circle appeared broken he reopened the oeuvre with East Coker and his brothers. It was not, however, until 1943 and only in the US that the four poems appeared as a unit. In England, where Eliot (as a director of the publishing house) controlled publication, they took an additional year to appear together in print

*   *   *

In Burnt Norton, Eliot took his cue from his romantic entanglements. In the three subsequent poems Eliot dealt with war and history. It has been said that Eliot's wartime poetry is less "metaphysical" than his prior work, more an attempt to understand the world than to get beyond it.[44] Who can doubt it: passing beyond the world is less interesting when the world seems intent on blowing itself up. Who cares about unborn children laughing among the leaves while those born perish in their tens and hundreds of thousands?

*   *   *

It is only with East Coker that the idea of the associated elements (codified in Little Gidding II.54-77) came into view. This change in theme introduced a new dynamism to the poems as the base elements of Heraclitus' system combine and recombine to compose the world of experience, and so, compared to the other poems, Burnt Norton seems stolid, lacking the motive force driving them.

So critics resort to Dante as an analogy. Dante wrote first and separately his Vita Nuova (describing his love and loss of Beatrice and concluding with his promise to write of her as no poet had written of a woman before) and his Comedy, where he carries through on that promise in three stages (Inferno, Purgatorio, Paradiso). Likewise, Four Quartets began with an earlier and originally separate poem (Burnt Norton) and follows through in three stages. East Coker begins with Burnt Norton's failure of immediate vision, introducing humility and repentance as the way beyond the initial failure. The Dry Salvages continues the journey introducing new concepts (Annunciation, Incarnation) in answer to the questions of East Coker. Little Gidding deploys these concepts in a new vision.[45]

*   *   *

Andrew Eliot, a man of property, learning and a dissenter in religion, left East Coker with his family in 1669 for the theologically more hospitable clime of Massachusetts. He met there, to his later chagrin, the notorious Judge Blood (one of Eliot's maternal ancestors) who embroiled him in the Salem witch trials. Years later (1692), he and eleven other men admitted in writing that they had been "sadly deluded and mistaken" fearing that they had shed "innocent blood."[46] This was the "original sin" of the Eliots in America.

Of puritan stock, Eliot was bred of people who sat in hard, straight-backed chairs calculating that the discomfort would cause them, sooner rather than later, to get up and *do* something. The war gave Eliot permission to have comforts. He had, for instance, to move from the room he rented in a Church Rectory to board in a suburban spare bedroom in the home of a widow with small children. That he gained weight from home cooking and had regular playtimes with the children, were "privations of war" and could not be helped.

His prayer life deepened and intensified, aided by the two nights a week spent in London as an air raid warden. All in all, the Eliot of East Coker is simply more likeable than the one who wrote Burnt Norton. More likeable, perhaps, but recognizable. When 12,000 copies of East Coker flew off the shelves, he wondered, with his wonted snobbery, if the public likes it, can it be any good?

*   *   *

War is a problem central to modernity. The philosophes of the Enlightenment had revamped political theory with an eye to peace. The religious wars of the Seventeenth Century were a recent memory and they saw religious disputes as a major source of civil and international strife. They wished to replace God, as arbiter of social relations, with reason. Reason, they thought, would bring peace.

But we, having survived the Twentieth Century, know better: making secular rule rational only made for bigger wars. Reason is an instrument only; bringing forth justice in the hands of just men, but despotism in the hands of tyrants. It cannot dissuade tyranny, only make it more efficient. So, a Greater War tread on the Great War's heels: a war heedless of civilian populations, a total war where armed and unarmed alike were subjected to extinction.

*   *   *

The philosophes' erred in locating the source of conflict *outside* the human psyche in religious ideology; wishfully thinking that religious toleration could marginalize fractious fanaticism. We, having seen secular ideology lead to wars that make religious conflicts resemble a Church social, recognize that any analysis of war that does not begin, "We have met the enemy and he is us" wastes good ink:

What causes wars, and what causes fightings among you? Is it not your passions that are at war in your members? You desire and do not have; so you kill. And you covet and cannot obtain; so you fight and wage war. You do not have, because you do not ask. You ask and do not receive, because you ask wrongly, to spend it on your passions. Unfaithful creatures! Do you not know that friendship with the world is enmity with God? Therefore whoever wishes to be a friend of the world makes himself an enemy of God. (James 4.1-4)

James claims war is an outward manifestation of an inward disorder, of misdirected desire. Anyone who has felt tempted to theft understands the cause of war, for war is theft writ large. Anyone who has felt the pull of greed knows what drives war: the desire to get something for nothing.

*   *   *

War requires concentration, a large group with a common interest that sets them afoul of another group in the competition for scarce resources. Warmongers quickly realized that the nation-state model provided a more efficient goad to war than religion ever had. The replacement of religious rationales for war by economic ones made the case for war stronger: people fight more readily for what they can see than for what they cannot.

Movement No. 1

In my beginning is my end. In succession
Houses rise and fall, crumble, are extended,
Are removed, destroyed, restored, or in their place

64

Is an open field, or a factory, or a by-pass.
Old stone to new building, old timber to new fires,
Old fires to ashes, and ashes to the earth
Which is already flesh, fur and faeces,
Bone of man and beast, cornstalk and leaf.
Houses live and die: there is a time for building
And a time for the wind to break the loosened pane
And to shake the wainscot where the field-mouse trots
And to shake the tattered arras woven with a silent motto. (I.1-13)

     We know the silent motto woven into the tattered arras because Eliot has already told us: "In my beginning is my end." Eliot's ashes rest in St. Michael's Church in East Coker, where a plague quotes the first and final lines of this poem: In my beginning is my end; In my end is my beginning.

*   *   *

     Mary of Scots had said, "In my end is my beginning," certain her execution would provoke Spain to invade England and restore the "true" Church. She felt herself a martyr and looked blithely past her death to a heavenly coronation. She was right that her death would start a war, but would have been appalled at the outcome.

     In a way, Mary's death gave birth to English history. Before, it had been the province of dusty chronicles chained to desks in the reference rooms of libraries. After the armada, English history became a subject to be profitably enacted on the stage. Having faced down the Spanish, the English hungered to know who they were. Shakespeare fed this newly-whetted appetite with two tetralogies of popular history plays, each crowned with a finale that gave the English their greatest royal hero (Henry V) and villain (Richard III).

*   *   *

     The critical voice speaks of Heraclitean flux. England remains England, not in spite of change but *because* of it. Change is not destruction, but replacement. Some houses are replaced by a larger version of themselves, others with "an open field, a factory, or a bypass." Thus England is renewed as the old passes away, replaced by the new. Everything falls to ash and returns to the earth "which is already flesh, fur and faeces." And the cycle begins again.

The cycle smacks of the conservation of energy. Nothing passes away without the new appearing. Old stone goes into new buildings, old timbers into new fires. And all of it returns to the earth from which it came. Eliot strikes a note of Ecclesiastes 3: a time for every purpose under heaven, a time to be born and a time to die, both corporately (families and nations) and individually.

That being said, there is another element to Ecclesiastes: "Vanity! Vanity! All is vanity." Not for nothing the ancient poet put these words in the mouth of a man known for great wealth and luminous intelligence. There is a time to die and be replaced by another, but, unlike the beast, unaware of death before it comes, the man is long bedeviled by death in the daily dread of its expectation.

*   *   *

Earth, as the element of this poem, represents temporal succession. Replacement permeates all of nature, but the change is most rapid and pronounced among humans. This is a consequence of language. The offspring of other species begin where their parents began: their generations running on a treadmill. Humans, through written language, accumulate knowledge passing it from generation to generation. Through writing, the dead speak to the living, their discourse tongued with fire. There are exceptions, but, for the most part, the wheel need be invented only once. In human culture, progress supplants evolution.

Progress differs from evolution by being *intentional*. The transition from hunting and gathering to agriculture and animal husbandry is no accident of genetic mutation, but a policy pursued over generations. We note this by attributing civilizations to *founders*, crystallizing the group's intention, pursued over generations in a single person. This avatar, whether Romulus, Achilles or Christ, embodies the group's identity, providing an ideal for corporate striving and a model for individuation.

* * *

   In time an old man's body replaces youthful grace. W. B. Yeats wrote in his poem "An acre of Grass:"
  Now strength of body goes;
Midnight, an old house
Where nothing stirs but a mouse (lines 4-6)
The field mouse trots across the wainscot in homage to Yeats who by it symbolized an old man's failing powers. Here it represents the King Lear senility of "Man come of Age."

* * *

In my beginning is my end. Now the light falls
Across the open field, leaving the deep lane
Shuttered with branches, dark in the afternoon,
Where you lean against a bank while a van passes,
And the deep lane insists on the direction
Into the village, in the electric heat
`Hypnotised. In a warm haze the sultry light
Is absorbed, not refracted, by grey stone.
The dahlias sleep in the empty silence.
Wait for the early owl. (I.14-23)
   As the clouds of war loomed ominously, Eliot made pilgrimage to his ancestral home to discover himself in that that had gone before.
   The sensual voice invites you to picture yourself on the road to the village of East Coker, a narrow lane that you must leave to let faster traffic (a van) past. Though it is afternoon, you walk in the shade (Eliot was, but a "shade" from his fiftieth birthday when he made his journey). The well-worn lane insists on bearing the poet to his place of burial. Time, however philosophically you assert its simultaneity moves you, as though

67

hypnotized, in only one direction. You are no ghost, but solid as stone, absorbing not refracting the light. Unlike the lotos rose, appearing only to disappear, the dahlia sleeps placidly in her bed. Unlike the thrush who, in Burnt Norton, bids you to enter the garden and bids you go, the owl, representing the wisdom of old age, never appears.

*   *   *

In that open field
If you do not come too close, if you do not come too close,
On a summer midnight, you can hear the music
Of the weak pipe and the little drum
And see them dancing around the bonfire
The association of man and woman
In daunsinge, signifying matrimonie —
A dignified and commodiois sacrament.
Two and two, necessarye coniunction,
Holding eche other by the hand or the arm
Whiche betokeneth concorde. (I.23-33)

The poet told us some houses fall to be "replaced" with an "open field" (EC I.4). No house greets his return, only an open field where it once might have stood. As all of Eliot's relations are in the US, only ghosts welcome him. He repairs to the open field at midnight and hears, in the distance, the music of a wedding feast, as ghosts dance in a sacramental celebration of union. A literary ghost addresses us:

And for as moche as by the association of a man and a woman in daunsinge may be signified matrimonic, I could in declarynge the dignitie and commoditie of that sacrament make intire volumes, if it were not so commonly knowen to all men that almost every frère lymitour carieth it writen in his bosome. (Sir Thomas Elyot, The Boke Named the Gouvernour, 1531)[47]

I cannot help imagining Eliot drawn to his ancestor's words by his own painful marital situation. By now, Vivienne's family had committed her to the "rest home" where she would spend the residue of her life. Eliot, come here fleeing the drumbeat of war, finds respite in the weak pipe and little drum.

Eliot, come here to escape the breakdown of community, finds solace among ghosts who, grasping each other hold worlds together. So, Eliot returns to the village his ancestors left to see their forebearers dance in sacramental joy. But the vision is no realer than that of the rose garden, the illusion persisting only if you do not come too close. Before the vision can come together, it must first fall apart.

*   *   *

Eliot's vision of connubial peace is only for those who do not come too close. The Boke Named the Gouvernour, detailing the education of a Sixteenth Century courtier, was not Sir Thomas' sole publication. He had also written a political tract warning Henry VIII not to divorce his good wife Katherine for Anne Boleyn, a piece of advice that, heeded, would have kept the Reformation out of England (The Pope had awarded Henry, for his attacks on Luther, the title "Defender of the Faith." In one of those ironies that live in history, Henry used this title to justify defending England from the Pope). Henry's lust destabilized England, as he was survived by three children from three wives; two Protestant and one Catholic. In the decade following his death, England veered drunkenly from Protestant to Catholic and back again as each heir took a turn on the throne.[48]

*   *   *

Round and round the fire
Leaping through the flames, or joined in circles,
Rustically solemn or in rustic laughter
Lifting heavy feet in clumsy shoes,
Earth feet, loam feet, lifted in country mirth
Mirth of those long since under earth
Nourishing the corn. Keeping time,
Keeping the rhythm in their dancing
As in their living in the living seasons
The time of the seasons and the constellations
The time of milking and the time of harvest

69

The time of the coupling of man and woman
And that of beasts. Feet rising and falling.
Eating and drinking. Dung and death. (I.33-46)

  The ghosts dance in circles, the cycles of nature. Most dance *around* the fire, others leap into the flames of lust. They are joined in generation, as beasts join to propagate their species. Their feet rise and fall in time to the music though they have, long since, gone beneath the earth, their bones fertilizing the corn that feeds the beasts who, in their turn, sustain human bodies. But time, for humans, is no mere cycle as it is for beasts. Human progress differentiates us from beasts who dance only *within* the turning cycle. To live only within the cycle is to share their "dung and death."

* * *

Dawn points, and another day
Prepares for heat and silence. Out at sea the dawn wind
Wrinkles and slides. I am here
Or there, or elsewhere. In my beginning. (I.47-50)

  The solemn critic's voice returns, but there is something new under the sun. The night ends as the Sun rises. The ghosts, like Hamlet's father, depart with the dawn (LG II.149). The dawn wind wafts in from the sea, the seat of the eternal. It does not matter where I am, for location in time and space is accidental. I am, wherever I am, at my beginning. My beginning is not a place in space and time, as time is ever on the move. Wherever I am, I am in the moment. The timeless moment is *now*.

Movement No. 2

What is the late November doing
With the disturbance of the spring
And creatures of the summer heat,
And snowdrops writhing under feet
And hollyhocks that aim too high
Red into grey and tumble down

70

Late roses filled with early snow?
Thunder rolled by the rolling stars
Simulates triumphal cars
Deployed in constellated wars
Scorpion fights against the Sun
Until the Sun and Moon go down
Comets weep and Leonids fly
Hunt the heavens and the plains
Whirled in a vortex that shall bring
The world to that destructive fire
Which burns before the ice-cap reigns. (II.51-68)

The above imagery has been described as "apocalyptic,"[49] but I find this designation more confusing than descriptive. Apocalyptic *is* the literary genre of choice for authors who see the world broken beyond human power to repair (as it is the humans, themselves, who are doing the breaking), but true apocalyptic does not despair. The Biblical book of Revelation, for all its dreadfulness, ends happily: the old world destroyed and replaced by a new and better. True apocalyptic transfers hope from human agency to divine intervention. No such expectation is here expressed.

*　　*　　*

I suspect we are better served to take our cue from the critical voice who, assessing the above, refers to it as "periphrastic" (II.68). Periphrasis, as a literary device, leaves its subject indirectly named. The second movement of Burnt Norton began with a like periphrasis describing the world as an axled tree made of a synthesis of vegetable (garlic), mineral (sapphires) and animal (clotted) matter. Here, we have juxtaposed two times of year corresponding to stages of human life: old age (late November) and youth (spring).

*　　*　　*

The disturbance of nature images an internal confusion. The above lines are not apocalyptic (i.e. they do not describe

71

motions in the outer world) but indirectly image the poet's confusion – they are inscape. Psychic disorder eludes the senses and, thus, the sensual voice describes it by referring to perceptible objects. The periphrasis is a consequence of its mode.

*   *   *

Asked of an individual, we question how the bafflement of youth (spring) turns into the bafflement of old age (late November). Eliot, as a youth, was taught wisdom came with age. Now he is old and none the wiser for it. He loved and married one woman in his youth and now is in love again. Asked historically, the Enlightenment rested on a simple premise: Man come of age. We no longer need God to save us: we have reason as our guide. But if that is so, why is the world going to war – again, and so soon. One could see it if people had had the time to forget the last great war, but they have not. An entire generation lost does not deter "reason."

*   *   *

That was a way of putting it – not very satisfactory:
A periphrastic study in a worn-out poetical fashion,
Leaving one still with the intolerable wrestle
With words and meanings. The poetry does not matter.
It was not (to start again) what one had expected.
What was to be the value of the long looked forward to,
Long hoped for calm, the autumnal serenity
And the wisdom of age? Had they deceived us
Or deceived themselves, the quiet-voiced elders,
Bequeathing us merely a receipt for deceit?
The serenity only a deliberate hebetude,
The wisdom only the knowledge of dead secrets
Useless in the darkness into which they peered
Or from which they turned their eyes. There is, it seems to us,
At best, only a limited value
In the knowledge derived from experience.
The knowledge imposes a pattern, and falsifies,

72

For the pattern is new in every moment
And every moment is a new and shocking
Valuation of all we have been. We are only undeceived
Of that which, deceiving, could no longer harm.
In the middle, not only in the middle of the way
But all the way, in a dark wood, in a bramble,
On the edge of a grimpen,† where is no secure foothold,
And menaced by monsters, fancy lights,
Risking enchantment. (II.67-93)

     The critical voice comments on the sensual voice's failure by asking directly (if prosily) the question he circumnavigated. Once you figure out what the sensual voice left unnamed you are at square one, and can *begin* to answer his question. The sensual voice added an unnecessary step to the process: "the intolerable wrestle with words and meaning." The critical voice, better placed to describing psychical processes, can frame the question directly, bringing us no nearer a solution, but leaving us no further from one.

*   *   *

     Is wisdom derived from of experience? Our gray-haired elders told us, when we were young, that they were wiser than we, and we, too inexperienced to know better, believed them.

     When I was ten, my great-uncle told me that if the reserve clause was ever abolished, the Yankees would win the World Series every year. I had not the historical perspective to realize that it was the 1960's when, with the reserve clause in place, the Yankees won the World Series every year. Nor did I know, as I do now, that, once the reserve clause was abolished, the Yankees could go a decade *without* winning it. My great-uncle won the argument, not because he was wiser than I, but because I could not judge the stronger argument.

     Is that the wisdom of old age: a flim-flam the old play on young, their ancient bodies which deny them vices exhibited as

---

† Per A. Conan Doyle (The Hounds of the Baskervilles), a bog or swamp.

monuments to virtue? Do they prey on children's lack of historical perspective to teach a wisdom that will later prove fallacious? Does experience teach anything we can rely on?

*   *   *

Pavlov's dog is the slave of experience: ring the bell and he salivates. He salivates not because he sees meat, but because the bell incites his expectation. Neither the bell nor his expectation provides meat, but he has come to associate the bell with meat and salivates in expectation. Each moment is new and as we impose our expectations, we falsify it, as if it were a past moment when the bell and meat coincided. Now is a new moment, when a new thing springs forth, but we will not perceive it if we are distracted by disappointed expectations.

*   *   *

We are only "undeceived" of that which deceiving can do no harm? I, for instance, have historical perspective on baseball's reserve clause. The reserve clause is a dead issue. No one can confuse me with a hypothetical argument because I know the outcome of its demise.

Experience, wise about dead issues of the past, may hinder our making wise choices now. Past results do not assure future success as we must choose in each new moment without knowing how our decision will manifest itself in the future. If I knew *then* what I know *now*, I might have chosen differently, but time's nature is that I *cannot* know then what I know now. Once I choose the moment recedes, irretrievably, into the past.

*   *   *

Dante began his Comedy:
Midway along the path that is our life
I awoke to find myself in a dark forest
Having lost the straight way. (Inferno 1.1-3)

74

providing the precedent for Eliot's comments on the middle way. Eliot, like Dante, refers to a dark wood. But here, there is an important additional clarification. Eliot tells us he is in the "middle way," but that he will go "all the way." He means not only physical death, but the death to self that is humility.

He told us that time (the lane) points insistently in one direction, to the village (death). Eliot never arrives there, stopping short at the open field. He is still in the "middle" way. He is at the beginning, on his way to a place that is endless.

*　　*　　*

Do not let me hear
Of the wisdom of old men, but rather of their folly,
Their fear of fear and frenzy, their fear of possession,
Of belonging to another, or to others, or to God.
The only wisdom we can hope to acquire
Is the wisdom of humility: humility is endless. (II.93-98)

Before God, all require forgiveness, but the world ever pumps us up, telling us, for its own purposes, that we are right, perceptive for thinking as we do (lest we change the channel). But this "rightness" is manipulation, the false reason of experience. To be alive is to be a fool. To be alive is to be constantly mindful of the *moment* which may be, if we are not watchful, the moment of sin. Humility is endless because only in humility does God exist. Only then are we in Its presence.

*　　*　　*

Yeats wrote in his A Prayer for Old Age:
GOD guard me from those thoughts men think
In the mind alone;
He that sings a lasting song
Thinks in a marrow-bone;
From all that makes a wise old man
That can be praised of all;
O what am I that I should not seem
For the song's sake a fool?

75

I pray -- for word is out
And prayer comes round again --
That I may seem, though I die old,
A foolish, passionate man.

Yeats died in 1939 and, in 1940 (the year of East Coker's publication), Eliot delivered the first Yeats memorial lecture in Dublin. In it he spoke of Yeats as the embodiment of his ideal of impersonality, a poet whose particularity made him universal.

*   *   *

The houses are all gone under the sea.
The dancers are all gone under the hill. (II.99-100)

The sensual voice concludes speaking of people and places buried. Houses, not subject to generation, lie under the burden of eternity (the sea). Dancers are buried by the succession of generations (the earth).

Movement No. 3

O dark dark dark. They all go into the dark,
The vacant interstellar spaces, the vacant into the vacant,
The captains, merchant bankers, eminent men of letters,
The generous patrons of art, the statesmen and the rulers,
Distinguished civil servants, chairmen of many committees,
Industrial lords and petty contractors, all go into the dark,
And dark the Sun and Moon, and the Almanach de Gotha
And the Stock Exchange Gazette, the Directory of Directors,
And cold the sense and lost the motive of action.
And we all go with them, into the silent funeral,
Nobody's funeral, for there is no one to bury. (III.101-111)

Eliot pokes fun at Milton's Samson Agonistes:
O dark, dark, dark amid the blaze of noon
The sun to me is dark
And silent as the moon
When she deserts the night
Hid in her vacant interlunar cave. (Samson Agonistes 80, 86-89)

Here interlunar is certainly a stroke of genius, but it is merely combined with 'vacant' and 'cave,' rather than receiving life from them. Thus it is not so unfair, as it might at first appear, to say that Milton writes English like a dead language. The criticism has been made with regard to his involved syntax. But a torturous style, when its peculiarity is aimed at precision (as with Henry James), is not necessarily a dead one; only when the complication is dictated by a demand of verbal music, instead of by any demand of sense.[50]

Eliot accuses Milton of introducing complication, not to *deliver* his message, but to ornament it. For living poetry, music and meaning must intertwine: there should be no rhyme without a reason.

*   *   *

The ode to darkness precedes a list of earthly professions, as if the dead were only empty suits of clothes. Like the list of famous men praised on All Saints Day (Ecclessiastius 44.1-10), these men are honored, not as human beings, but as social *functionaries:* they are praised for their *usefulness.*

Society requires of its people certain functions to ensure its survival and prosperity. To span more than a single generation, the people must generate children to replace the citizens who die, renewing the people. To prosper, the people must produce goods and services, contributing to the economy. To survive, the people must be warriors, beating back the predations of other tribes and peoples. To be wise, the people must cultivate science, art and religion. Society, recognizing its need for these functions, praises those who serve them. Society insists we take pride in our accomplishments (as lambs lying proudly on society's altar), and find "meaning" in losing ourselves for the sake of many.

Eliot's intent becomes manifest as his list descends from occupations to lists. The Almanach de Gotha, for instance, is a list of English Royals. He tops it all off with a parody of Hamlet contemplating suicide:

Thus conscience does make cowards of us all;
And thus the native hue of resolution

Is sicklied o'er with the pale cast of thought,
And enterprises of great pith and moment
With this regard their currents turn awry,
And lose the name of action. (Hamlet Act 3, scene 1)
Hamlet, desiring release from the burden of vengeance, thinks to
turn his knife on himself. He does not do it, finding in thinking
the substitute for doing. Likewise, no corpse attends the silent
funeral. The deceased could not get the day off from work.

*   *   *

I said to my soul, be still, and let the dark come upon you
Which shall be the darkness of God. As, in a theatre,
The lights are extinguished, for the scene to be changed
With a hollow rumble of wings, with a movement of darkness on
darkness,
And we know that the hills and the trees, the distant panorama
And the bold imposing facade are all being rolled away —
Or as, when an underground train, in the tube, stops too long between
stations
And the conversation rises and slowly fades into silence
And you see behind every face the mental emptiness deepen
Leaving only the growing terror of nothing to think about;
Or when, under ether, the mind is conscious but conscious of nothing
(III.112-122)
 "Be still and know that I am God" (Psalm 46.10). Stillness
counsels humility. This darkness, the true darkness, heralds
God's approach. It shows up the busyness of the world as
idleness; the death it fears, a fevered dream. To leave the
darkness, take it into yourself, allow it to own you.

*   *   *

 Eliot follows with three darknesses, each darker than the
last. The first he steals from Shakespeare:
Our revels now are ended. These our actors,
As I foretold you, were all spirits and
Are melted into air, into thin air:

And, like the baseless fabric of this vision,
The cloud-capp'd towers, the gorgeous palaces,
The solemn temples, the great globe itself,
Yea all which it inherit, shall dissolve
And, like this insubstantial pageant faded,
Leave not a rack behind. We are such stuff
As dreams are made on, and our little life
Is rounded with a sleep. (The Tempest Act 4 Scene 1)
Eliot speaks of the darkness as scenery is changed in the theatre.
Shakespeare has Prospero speak of even "the great globe itself,"
passing away leaving not a rack behind. Ironically, though
unaware he is a character in a play, Prospero knows the name of
the theatre in which he is being enacted.

*   *   *

Caesar Augustus asked, as he lay dying:
If I have played my part well, applaud as I exit the stage. (Suetonius,
Twelve Caesars, Life of Augustus, 99)
He knew, only too well, life as farce. The first darkness is that of
worldly occupations. It is the eclipse of the list. To identify with
your worldly role is not to be a self, but to be a costume an actor
wears. Not even the actor, but only his garb.

*   *   *

The second darkness Eliot takes from Burnt Norton:
Nor darkness to purify the soul
Emptying the sensual with deprivation
Cleansing affection from the temporal.
Neither plenitude nor vacancy. Only a flicker
Over the strained time-ridden faces
Distracted from distraction by distraction
Filled with fancies and empty of meaning
Tumid apathy with no concentration (BN III.96-103)
The lights in the subway are bright enough to let us occupy
ourselves with book or newspaper, but it is neither true light nor
darkness. We see this when the train, stuck between stations,

79

leaves the commuters to their anxiety. Not that anxiety is strange to them, but that they, momentarily, lack a distraction from it, that, for the moment, their thoughts loom before them. This is the second darkness, the darkness of the soul.

*   *   *

The final darkness comes from the Love song of J. Alfred Prufrock:
Let us go then, you and I,
When the evening is spread out against the sky
Like a patient etherized upon a table;
The evening darkness, spread out against the sky, is mindful of its presence and nothing else. This is the darkness of God.

*   *   *

I said to my soul, be still, and wait without hope
For hope would be hope for the wrong thing; wait without love,
For love would be love of the wrong thing; there is yet faith
But the faith and the love and the hope are all in the waiting.
Wait without thought, for you are not ready for thought:
So the darkness shall be the light, and the stillness the dancing.
(III.124-128)
He advises his soul on the Theological Virtues: Hope, Love and Faith (1 Corinthians 13.13), telling her to wait, for waiting is humility. However wisely I choose what I hope for, I must hope for the wrong thing. However wisely I choose what I love, I must love the wrong thing. Faith is not what I choose, but a God-given gift. Faith, Hope and Love are not in what we do, but are in the waiting:
I wait for the LORD, my soul waits, and in his word I hope;
my soul waits for the LORD more than watchmen for the morning,
more than watchmen for the morning. (Psalm 130.5-6)

*   *   *

The Theological virtues correspond to the three darknesses:

1) Treating worldly occupations as a costume worn to a masquerade is waiting without hope as we despair of earthly salvation.
2) Living without distracting oneself from oneself is waiting without love as we despair of earthly things as a source of durable joy.
3) Faith is to be simply present as "the evening is spread out against the sky."

It is not for faith to determine the times and seasons, but to discern and follow them (Ecclesiastes 3.1). This is the meaning of humility, waiting and discipleship. One never becomes master because the master is in heaven and we wait to discern Its will to follow It in love. God is a mystery and, in waiting, we become present to that which cannot be grasped.

* * *

Whisper of running streams, and winter lightning.
The wild thyme unseen and the wild strawberry,
The laughter in the garden, echoed ecstasy
Not lost, but requiring, pointing to the agony
Of death and birth. (III.129-133)

The sensual voice returns with natural images, images of motion in earth and sky, of herbs and of fruit, of the garden of Burnt Norton and its ghosts unable to contain their laughter. The timeless moment is not lost with the returning of time, but its remembrance requires a birth that is death. The Apostle asks:
Unfaithful creatures! Do you not know that friendship with the world is enmity with God? (James 4.4)
To be born to spirit is to die to the world, just as to be born in the world is to die to spirit.

* * *

You say I am repeating
Something I have said before. I shall say it again.

81

Shall I say it again? In order to arrive there,
To arrive where you are, to get from where you are not,
You must go by a way wherein there is no ecstasy.
In order to arrive at what you do not know
You must go by a way which is the way of ignorance.
In order to possess what you do not possess
You must go by the way of dispossession.
In order to arrive at what you are not
You must go through the way in which you are not.
And what you do not know is the only thing you know
And what you own is what you do not own
And where you are is where you are not. (III.133-146)

People learn by repetition. Repeat a lie often enough and the will wearies its resistance: even one who knows better will begin to believe it. The echo chamber is often the best teacher.

Eliot ends the movement quoting John of the Cross:

In order to arrive at having pleasure in everything, Desire to have pleasure in nothing. In order to arrive at possessing everything, Desire to possess nothing. In order to arrive at being everything, Desire to be nothing. In order to arrive at knowing everything, Desire to know nothing. In order to arrive at that wherein thou hast no pleasure, Thou must go by a way wherein thou hast no pleasure. In order to arrive at that which thou knowest not, Thou must go by a way that thou knowest not. In order to arrive at that which thou possessest not, Thou must go by a way that thou possessest not. In order to arrive at that which thou art not, Thou must go through that which thou art not.[51]

Wittgenstein, who apparently had a pithy phrase for every occasion, said,

There is also no problem where the solution can be expected only from a sort of revelation. To revelation there corresponds no question.[52]

This saying, to my mind, merely repeats the wisdom of Isaiah:

"Seek the LORD while he may be found, call upon him while he is near; let the wicked forsake his way, and the unrighteous man his thoughts; let him return to the LORD, that he may have mercy on him, and to our God, for he will abundantly pardon. For my thoughts are not your thoughts, neither are your ways my ways, says the LORD. For as the heavens are higher than the earth, so are my ways higher than your ways and my thoughts than your thoughts. "For as the rain

and the snow come down from heaven, and return not thither but water
the earth, making it bring forth and sprout, giving seed to the sower
and bread to the eater, so shall my word be that goes forth from my
mouth; it shall not return to me empty, but it shall accomplish that
which I purpose, and prosper in the thing for which I sent it. (Isaiah
55.6-11)
No problem corresponds to revelation because God does not
reveal Itself in answer to human questions or to fulfill human
desires. As high as Heaven is above the earth, so revelation
transcends earth-bound questions. Thus, our journey to God
begins in darkness, in surrendering our own questions in order
to hear God's answers.

Movement No. 4

      The fourth movement lyric is a prayer in the mode of the
metaphysical poets, of which John Donne's "Good Friday 1613,
Riding Westward" provides an example.[53] The title says it all. In
a traditional Anglican Church the Altar is affixed to the eastern
wall so that, at the consecration of the Eucharist, every eye is
turned towards the sunrise, the image of Christ. But Donne, on
this Good Friday, rides west, in anger and despair:
LET man's soul be a sphere, and then, in this,
Th' intelligence that moves, devotion is ;
And as the other spheres, by being grown
Subject to foreign motion, lose their own,
And being by others hurried every day,
Scarce in a year their natural form obey ;
Pleasure or business, so, our souls admit
For their first mover, and are whirl'd by it.
Hence is't, that I am carried towards the west,
This day, when my soul's form bends to the East.
If the heaven and the soul, both made by God, bear the same
shape, then, as the angels move the heavenly spheres, so the
devotion to God should rightly move the soul. Sin supplants the
rightful mover and, through "business or pleasure," enslaves her
to worldly concerns as to a foreign power (Romans 7.15-23). The

soul is so diverted from her natural bent that "scarce in a year" she conforms to her natural shape. Donne, himself, provides the example: he rides west on Good Friday when his soul should look east.

*   *   *

The lyric is in five stanzas of five lines each: five being the number of wounds Christ suffered on the Cross.[54]
The wounded surgeon plies the steel
That questions the distempered part;
Beneath the bleeding hands we feel
The sharp compassion of the healer's art
Resolving the enigma of the fever chart. (IV.147-151)
A surgeon wounds *us* to restore our health, but here *he* is bloodied. The contradiction is only apparent as the surgeon's work is two-fold: having bled himself, he now turns his scalpel (the Cross) on us, questioning our distempered part (our sins). Thus, sin is not our nature, but a second nature turning us away from our true, created nature. This second nature Christ (as surgeon) extirpates without killing the patient.

*   *   *

In ancient times, Priests were healers, sacrificing sheep and cattle, offering them to God, day by day, year by year, to atone for the sins of the people. The Church took over this image (Hebrew 9.1-15) seeing Christ as Priest *and* paschal lamb, the one offering the sacrifice and his victim.

The New Testament writers, though opposed to animal sacrifice, failed to foresee a "victory" of Christianity so complete as to overthrow the sacrificial altars. This left their successors, the Schoolmen, the problem of explaining the atonement when the New Testament's primary metaphor was no more.

It was no accident that the effort to formulate a theological explanation of Christ's death began with Anselm (c. 1033-1109). Anselm, as philosopher, had tools to deconstruct animal sacrifice as a metaphor, and, as poet, had the skills to

84

replace it with the image of God as a feudal landlord and we, as His tenants, arrears with our rent (good works) and, larcenous to boot (sin). The landlord must either:

1) Turn us off the land
2) Make us remit the back rent and pay for our theft.
3) Remit the debt himself.

Option 2 is unworkable because no human being can offer a sufficient sacrifice. So God remitted the debt through His son, the God-man. Christ's death ransoms the tenants restoring the landlord's honor.

This idea had a long and useful life, but, when feudalism ended, it too went stale. By his image of the hospital, Eliot attempts create an analogy for modern times.[55]

*   *   *

When Jesus saw his mother, and the disciple whom he loved standing near, he said to his mother, "Woman, behold, your son!" Then he said to the disciple, "Behold, your mother!" And from that hour the disciple took her to his own home. (John 19.26-27)

Jesus commanded his Mother (Holy Mother Church) to look at him. The Church's authority rests on Her vision of the Crucified Jesus. Then Jesus gave his Holy Mother into the care of his disciple (the individual Christian), giving him or her care of the Church, the sacramental community of the faithful.

Our only health is the disease
If we obey the dying nurse
Whose constant care is not to please
But to remind of our, and Adam's curse,
And that, to be restored, our sickness must grow worse. (IV.152-156)

The previous verse described sin as an "enigma." The heart, deceitful above all things (Jeremiah 17.9), desires to do evil but be seen as good, believing it better to appear just than to be just. Thus, when confronted with their sins, the world nailed Jesus to the Cross to punish his presumption in pointing out its injustice, an injustice ironically confirmed by their act. Only those who take the bitter medicine of accepting their sinfulness have possibility of cure. Our only health lies in the disease, in

85

accepting that we are, ourselves, sinners and helping other to see and correct their sins.

To this end we are given the support of the "dying nurse" (the Church) who, looking to the Cross, makes her care not to please but remind us of our and Adam's curse.

*   *   *

The whole earth is our hospital
Endowed by the ruined millionaire,
Wherein, if we do well, we shall
Die of the absolute paternal care
That will not leave us, but prevents us everywhere. (IV.157-161)

Who is the "ruined millionaire? Is it Adam?[56] I think not. Dante interviews Adam in heaven: he has escaped Hell (Inferno 4.55) and rests among the blessed (Paradiso 26.82-142).

To make this point I must call Eliot to task. He wrote, concerning the final canto of Inferno:

The last canto is probably the most difficult on the first reading. The vision of Satan may seem grotesque, especially if we have fixed in our minds the curly-haired Byronic hero of Milton; it is too like a Satan in a fresco in Siena. Certainly no more than the Divine Spirit can the Essence of Evil be confined to one form and place; and I confess that I tend to get from Dante the impression of a Devil suffering like the human damned souls; whereas I feel that the kind of suffering experienced by the Spirit of Evil should be represented as utterly different.[57]

Eliot takes issue with the mode of Satan's punishment and, having shared his qualms, I understand them. Dante took a peculiar joy in tripping up his readers.

Satan, for his rebellion against God, was thrown down from heaven with so great a force, he fell not *to* earth, but *through* it. His fall excavated the pit of Hell and the dirt thrown up became the mount of Purgatory. Wedged in the center of the earth, where gravity changes its polarity, Satan found himself in a pool where the river Cocytus flowed into the newly-formed chasm. He flapped his great wings to lift himself out of the mud generating an icy blast that froze the Cocytus, trapping him in ice (Inferno 34.121-126). To lift himself out, he flapped his wings again and again, each time freezing the Cocytus and locking himself in more tightly. To release himself, Satan need only stop his wings, allowing the Cocytus to melt. Why does he not remained unexplained until, over sixty cantos later, Beatrice spills the beans:

"But, because on Earth, throughout your schools
They teach that Angels are able
To know, recollect and to will,
I will speak further, that you may see
The clear truth that is confused down below
By the equivocations of teaching.
These substances, since first they rejoiced
In the face of God, from which naught is hid
Have not turned their eyes from it,
So that their sight is never interrupted
By a new object, therefore they need not
Search for a divided concept." (Paradiso 29.70-81)

The Angels, created to dwell "where all "when" and "wheres" converge" (Paradiso 29.12), have no *memories*. In God's presence everything and everywhere is immediately present to them: they have no need for memory and it is an aspect of their perfection not to have one. Satan, fallen into time, found himself lying in a lake. He flapped his wings to lift himself out of it and the lake froze. Each time he flapped his wings was, as far as he knew, the first time and this first time was infinitely repeated. Satan's punishment provides the precedent for the punishment of all the damned.

Satan, not Adam, is the "ruined millionaire."

If this is so, then what is the "paternal care" threatening to kill us? We know Adam as our father by flesh. We know Abraham as our father by spirit. How is Satan our father? He is the father of lies (John 8.44, Inferno 23.144).

Lies persuade and dissuade, lead to pleasure and help us avoid pain. Satan first tempted Jesus by questioning his belly. When pleasure and pain determine our actions, our life is no longer our own. This is why Jesus answered, "It was written that, 'No one can be sustained by only bread, but by every word issuing from the mouth of God '" (Matthew 4.3-4). Jesus rejects Satan's temptation, but not by his own wisdom (giving Satan the opportunity to challenge his ego), but by Moses'. This is humility.

The "paternal care" is the satanic "endowment" which tells us that wisdom comes with age and appearing just is better than justice itself. This "wisdom" prevents us everywhere.

*   *   *

The chill ascends from feet to knees,
The fever sings in mental wires.
If to be warmed, then I must freeze
And quake in frigid purgatorial fires
Of which the flame is roses, and the smoke is briars. (IV.162-166)

The first line alludes to the Hostess' speech in Henry V, describing the death of Sir John Falstaff:

So he cried out, "God, God, God!" three or four times. Now I, to comfort him, bid him he should not think of God; I hoped there was no need to trouble himself with any such thoughts yet. So he bade me lay more clothes on his feet. I put my hand into the bed and felt them, and they were as cold as any stone; then I felt to his knees, and they were as cold as any stone; and so upward and upward, and all was as cold as any stone. (Henry V Act 2 Scene 3)

As Falstaff lay dying, his mind turned to God, but his Hostess, trying to comfort him, told him there was no need to trouble himself with such thoughts -- *yet.*

*   *   *

The second line alludes to Guido Montelfeltro, who compares Pope Boniface VIII to Constantine and himself to Pope Sylvester:

As Constantine summoned Sylvester
From Mount Soracte to cure his leprosy,
So this one sought me for his physician
To cure the burning fever of his pride. (Inferno 27.94-96)

Guido, like the Hostess, is a bad physician. Constantine called Sylvester seeking a good (a cure for his leprosy). Boniface called on Guido seeking an evil (advice on how to injure his fellow Christian). For good to result from both transactions, one request must be honored (Constantine's), and the other, refused (Boniface's). Guido, heeding Boniface's lie that he can absolve a sin before it is done, aids Boniface and awakes in Hell.

Guido, angry and confused, trusted religious authority – and went to Hell. He tried to quit his evil ways before it was too late – and went to Hell. His son, Buonconte, a sinner until the hour of his death, confessed his sin and escaped Hell, waking from death in Purgatory. He did not confess to a Priest or Pope, but to Our Lady, who heard in secret. The moral is that repentance (humility) alone is the path to heaven, but more than that:

And let not people be so confident
In judging – as he who, in the fields,
Counts the ears of corn before they ripen.
For I have seen the briar, all winter through,
Show its rough and prickly stem,
And then, bear a rose at its height.
And I have seen a ship sail straight and swift
Over the sea, its whole course through
Only to founder as it enters its harbor. (Paradiso 13.130-138)

We would think Guido, bemoaning his sins before his death, had finally found the right course, but he sank at the mouth of the harbor. And, that Buonconte, giving his sins no thought before his last moments, is a briar condemned to burn in unquenchable fires, when it is he who bears the rose.

*   *   *

Yet dare I almost be glad, I do not see
That spectacle of too much weight for me.
Who sees Gods face, that is self-life, must die;
What a death were it then to see God die?
It made His own lieutenant, Nature, shrink,
It made His footstool crack, and the sun wink.

Could I behold those hands, which span the poles
And tune all spheres at once, pierced with those holes?
Could I behold that endless height, which is
Zenith to us and our antipodes,
Humbled below us ? or that blood, which is
The seat of all our soul's, if not of His,
Made dirt of dust, or that flesh which was worn
By God for His apparel, ragg'd and torn ?
If on these things I durst not look, durst I
On His distressed Mother cast mine eye,
Who was God's partner here, and furnish'd thus
Half of that sacrifice which ransom'd us?
Though these things as I ride be from mine eye,
They're present yet unto my memory,
For that looks towards them ; and Thou look'st towards me,
O Saviour, as Thou hang'st upon the tree. (John Donne, Good Friday
1613, Riding Westward)

Donne's lines are a monument to ambivalence. He is *almost* glad he did not behold the crucifixion. God is his hope for eternal life, what despair would he have suffered to see Him die? Nature, itself, was riven by the sight of its Creator "pierced with those holes." Could he have borne seeing the one who, by right, should be lifted infinitely high, raised upon the Cross to die? Could he have borne seeing the "justice" done, by which our salvation was won? He is *almost* glad to have missed the sight of the crucifixion, as its *echo* brings terror to his mind. And so Christ peers down from his Cross on Donne's receding form as he spurs his horse away.

*   *   *

The dripping blood our only drink,
The bloody flesh our only food:
In spite of which we like to think
That we are sound, substantial flesh and blood —
Again, in spite of that, we call this Friday good. (IV.167-172)

Eliot's contradiction is less dramatic, but more spiritually frightful. Donne, imagining the "sign of Jonah" (Matthew 12.39-

41), has the good sense to run. Eliot describes a double-minded piety that:

        a)   Recognizes "the dripping blood as our only drink, the bloody flesh our only food."

        b)   But thinks, simultaneously, that we are "sound, substantial, flesh and blood."

No one can serve two masters. Either the sacrament is the medicine of eternal life, or it is food for the body supporting power, position, wealth and what they buy. If the latter, then one would be wise to mount one's horse (the body) and flee the Cross like the plague. Eliot laments that many "Christians" want to possess both the sacraments and the world.

            *   *   *

We return to Guido and his son, Buonconte. Guido loses his soul, believing a prelate who, having lost sight of the Cross, tells him he can have his cake and eat it too. Buonconte, dying on the battle field, finds his, as he contritely confessing his sins to Our Lady. Donne, fleeing the Cross, cannot escape Christ's eye and may, one day, turn to face him, but what can save those smug souls who, calling this Friday good, trust the Church to save their souls?

Movement No. 5

So here I am, in the middle way, having had twenty years —
Twenty years largely wasted, the years of l'entre deux guerres
Trying to use words, and every attempt
Is a wholly new start, and a different kind of failure
Because one has only learnt to get the better of words
For the thing one no longer has to say, or the way in which
One is no longer disposed to say it. And so each venture
Is a new beginning, a raid on the inarticulate
With shabby equipment always deteriorating
In the general mess of imprecision of feeling,
Undisciplined squads of emotion. And what there is to conquer

91

By strength and submission, has already been discovered
Once or twice, or several times, by men whom one cannot hope
To emulate – but there is no competition –
There is only the fight to recover what has been lost
And found and lost again and again: and now, under conditions
That seem unpropitious. But perhaps neither gain nor loss.
For us, there is only the trying. The rest is not our business. (V172-189)

Eliot claims he had mostly wasted the twenty years between the two wars. What can he mean? It was a very eventful period:

1) He had written his masterpiece, The Waste Land, and other acclaimed books of poetry.
2) From 1922-1939 he edited the Criterion, a quarterly literary journal.
3) Helped found a publishing house which had nurtured many young writers.
4) Written critical essays that made him a literary arbiter.
5) He had changed both nationality and religion.
6) He had lectured at universities both in England and the United States.

So, why does he say he had wasted his time?

*   *   *

We can interpret this "middle way" in Dantean terms:
Midway along the path that is our life
I awoke to find myself in a dark forest
Having lost the straight way. (Inferno 1.1-3)
The "midway" Dante means is middle age. His sun has completed its ascent and is declining, inexorably, towards its horizon. This jolts him from sleep and he realizes that he has lost his way. Dante was 35 and Eliot, here, is 52. Eliot is beyond the initial recognition, the dawning of awareness Dante describes. He, looking back on the activities of the previous decades, sees only vanity and chasing the wind.

92

*   *   *

How does one "get the better of words?" Or, better yet, does one ever get the better of words? Having never taken their measure, I would not know. I must take Eliot's word that one gets the better of words only for "the thing one no longer has to say or the way in which one is no longer disposed to say it." I do, however, recognize this saying as an avowal of a Socratic ignorance. Humility is endless because it is always at the beginning.

*   *   *

In an interview, Eliot commenting on his "move from a narrower to a larger audience," cited two reasons:
1) His writing drama contributed to simplifying his language, as drama converses with the audience. Though he continued saying complex things, he had gotten into the habit of saying them more simply.
2) Experience and maturity allow the poet a choice of *how* to say a thing. Obscurity fogs the young poet's work by his having either to frame an abstruse point confusingly or not at all. The young poet still struggles with his medium. A greater command of words and rhythms allows the mature poet greater flexibility of expression.[58]

*   *   *

As progress is the property of the collective, so art, at the intersection of individual experience and acquired technique, never improves. Art merely returns over and over again to the same ground differing means at its disposal. This not to say progress does not change the soul. Slave-based and industrial economies produce different human types, but that this change amounts to little more than differing styles of clothes. Read Plato.

As a result, the artist does not "contribute" to art as a scientist offers a monograph on which others may build. An artist changes, with a poem or painting, the entire of art. A new vision recasts the whole tradition in a new light. As there is no progress, there is no competition: art does not advance, but rises, like a phoenix, from the ashes.

*　　*　　*

Poetry, like religion, is *aspirational,* thus the "wisdom" of old men is its antithesis. Such "wisdom," born of self-satisfaction, is an accumulation of a wealth one may rest in, saying, "You have ample goods laid up for many years; take your ease, eat, drink, be merry" (Luke 12.19). We live towards the ideal, because religion, like art, is a *striving* and never an accomplishment.

Each "achievement" is but a new kind of failure pushing the gap between aspiration and satisfaction further out. There can be no final conquest as each victory leaves a larger land unconquered. Humility is endless because it is never satisfied. Regardless of its achievements, it is an unworthy servant having done only her duty (Luke 17.10)

*　　*　　*

Home is where one starts from. As we grow older
The world becomes stranger, the pattern more complicated
Of dead and living. (V.190-192)

Here we begin our segue from earth to water, from East Coker to the Dry Salvages. Home *is* where we start from. Eliot started from St. Louis, Missouri. The Dry Salvages will leave England, the land of his choosing, and cross an ocean to the land of his birth. This is but one of the ways the pattern is complicated: we are born to live one life, but may *choose* to live another.

*　　*　　*

In our youth, those who love us surround us, and, if we are lucky, the scythe of death does not cut too close. But,

94

growing older, death becomes a familiar acquaintance. To live long is to bury most of those we love, and end surrounded by comparative strangers who do not share our memories, or culture, or, seemingly, our language. Growing older, the companions of youth grow fewer and more precious as those we know and love recede into the earth.

*   *   *

Not the intense moment
Isolated, with no before and after,
But a lifetime burning in every moment
And not the lifetime of one man only
But of old stones that cannot be deciphered.
There is a time for the evening under starlight,
A time for the evening under lamplight
(The evening with the photograph album). (V.192-199)

Eliot perhaps gave a false impression earlier:
Time past and time future
Allow but a little consciousness.
To be conscious is not to be in time
But only in time can the moment in the rose-garden,
The moment in the arbour where the rain beat,
The moment in the draughty church at smokefall
Be remembered; involved with past and future.
Only through time time is conquered. (BN II.82-89)

We, perhaps misled, supposed Eliot disparaged time past and future in the name of the timeless moment, that, for him, time has value merely as the anteroom of eternity. Here, Eliot offers clarification: the timeless moment, remembered in time, *shapes* time. We remember timeless moments for the same reason we strike flint over kindling: to set that which is cold alight.

Nor is the now-moment to be isolated from before and after, our life is not the lifetime of one man only, but that of indecipherable headstones. No man is an island, entire to himself, but part of a greater continent and all our lives, past, present and future, merge into a single story.

*   *   *

Love is most nearly itself
When here and now cease to matter. (V.200-201)

Too often quibblers question love without an object. Eliot understood this as well as anyone. Natural love is preferential. We love this person because she reminds us of that we most enjoy in ourselves. We hate that person because he reminds us of that we most hate about ourselves. Love and hate are born in the funhouse mirror of the ego, only learning, later if ever, that the other has a self beyond our feelings about them. Eliot's point is that love is most authentic when it transcends self-identification, when love is no longer a reflection of the ego.

We must radically invert the quibbler's question: here and now cease to matter not in terms of the object, but of the *subject.* I love most worthily when I do not judge whether the object is loveable. I willingly concede that such a love may not be humanly possible, but the quibbler must explain why love must be degraded into what is humanly possible. Moreover, if we do not *aspire* to a higher love, how can we know what is humanly possible?

*   *   *

Old men ought to be explorers
Here or there does not matter (V.202-203)

In Inferno 26 and 27 Dante and Virgil converse with two old men. In Inferno 26 Virgil interviews Ulysses who, rather than returning home from Troy confesses:
Not tender love for a son, nor duty
To an aged father, nor love owed
Penelope, to make her happy,
Would quench my burning wish
To know the world and experience
All human vices and worth. (Inferno 26.94-99)
Ulysses sheds human bonds to pursue his quest for universal knowledge. He, moreover, risked his remaining crews' lives, exhorting them:

96

"Brothers," I said, "who have endured
        A hundred thousand perils
        Striving to reach the west,
Do not deny yourselves, in the brief vigil left to your senses,
        The experience of that lying beyond the sun,
        In the world known as unpeopled.
Consider the seed from which you grew: you are Greeks!
        Not born to live like mindless brutes
        But to pursue virtue and knowledge" (Inferno 26.112-120)
Is this what Eliot means by old men should be explorers? Clearly
not. Ulysses' mad flight is a cautionary tale ending in shipwreck.
Dante's tale begins with his surviving a metaphorical shipwreck
(Inferno 1.22-27). Approaching the Mountain, three beasts warn
him and he retreats (Inferno 1.16-62), but Ulysses, warned by the
pillars of Hercules (Inferno 26.108-109), exhorts his men to sail
impiously on. After months at sea, he approaches Mount
Purgatory. But the mountain has a secret: at its peak lies the
Garden of Eden which is forbidden humankind (Genesis 3.24).
He says, describing his final vision:
When, before us rose, dark in the distance,
        A mountain which appeared to me
        To be the tallest that I had ever seen.
Our joy quickly changed to weeping
        For from the new land a whirlwind arose
        And battered at the bow of the ship.
Three times it whirled her within its waters,
        At the fourth, it lifted the stern aloft
        And our prow plunged deep, as pleased Another,
Until the sea had closed over us. (Inferno 26.133-142)
The pilgrim, safely arrived at the foot of the same Mountain,
said:
At last we touched that lonely shore
        That has never seen its waters sailed
        By one who returned to tell the tale.
There, as Another willed he girded me. (Purgatorio 1.130-133)
Dante is, himself, Ulysses' counter example, travelling at
Heaven's invitation and heeding Heaven's warnings he safely
arrives where Ulysses disastrously aspired to be.

*   *   *

In Inferno 27, we meet Ulysses' opposite, the crafty Guido Montelfeltro who, cautiously refrained from exploration:
When I saw that I had reached an age
That I, like everyman,
Must lower the sails and gather the lines,
I sorrowed for what I had once found pleasant;
Repentant and confessed, I surrendered
And, alas, it would have worked!" (Inferno 27.79-84)
Ulysses sought a deeper communion in the wrong way, in the pursuit of knowledge for self-gratification. Guido side-stepped Ulysses' peril to fall into another: rather than seek a deeper communion, he trusts the collective (the monastery and Pope) to save him. That he ends in the same Hell as Ulysses evidences his error.

The pursuit of a deeper communion is not the ego driven pursuit of our desires (for even of so lofty a thing as knowledge), nor is it to sink more deeply into the collective. Rather:
We must be still and still moving
Into another intensity
For a further union, a deeper communion
Through the dark cold and the empty desolation,
The wave cry, the wind cry, the vast waters
Of the petrel and the porpoise. (V.204-208)
Am I repeating myself? May I repeat myself? The idea here is the same as in Burnt Norton movement 5: coextension. The wheel of Dharma revolves not only at its hub, but, in contact with the earth, moves through space and time. Thus the wheel is both still (it turns around the hub, which is *not* in motion) and, in contact with the earth, moves through time and space. This double motion will reemerge in The Dry Salvages as incarnation: the impossible union.

Ulysses is moving, but is not still. Guido is still, but unmoving. Like Dante, Eliot resorts to images of the sea. He also suggests means to navigation. The petrel (Peter and the Church)

98

and porpoise (Christ)[59] are the compass enabling us to cross the desolate deep.

The owl, though promised, never arrived. The petrel, the wisdom of humility, alone is sustaining.

*   *   *

In my end is my beginning. (V.208)

Dante's Inferno ends in inversion: he climbs *down* Satan's shank to discover, on the other side of the world, that he has climbed *up* (Inferno 34.70-120). He is in a new hemisphere, greeted by stars not seen by living humans since the fall. Eliot began East Coker quoting Mary of Scots backwards (In my beginning is my end) and ended with the quotation flipped right-side up (In my end is my beginning). He began it awaiting an absent owl, and ended with wisdom arriving on petrel's wings.

With Mary of Scots' words righted we see the end of East Coker is the beginning of The Dry Salvages.

The Church of Notre Dame de la Gard above Marseilles

The Dry Salvages

If life is lived forward and understood backwards, then in East Coker, Eliot stood on the threshold of old age looking forward, deciding what kind of old man he would become: a wise man or a fool. Growing up, he was told the laurel of wisdom is the crown of old age: only fools say otherwise. Eliot resolved to become a fool. Fools learn through pain as wise men explain their suffering away. As the "wisdom" of old age is invincible, Eliot decided to become vulnerable.

In The Dry Salvages Eliot turns to the past, recollecting how he became who he is. It begins in the St. Louis of his birth, moves to his childhood summer home, through his years of education and ends with his flight from the new world to the old to make his name as a man of letters.

*　　*　　*

Though Dante and Eliot were peregrine poets their similarities end at their native borders: they are exiles for opposite reasons. Dante was at the Papal Court on a diplomatic mission when his faction in Florence fell from power and he was denied return on pain of death. Eliot, on the other hand, went to Europe on scholarship and, debarred immediate return by the outbreak of World War I, *chose* to settle in England. One's exile was forced, the other's voluntary.

Dante never relinquished Florentine citizenship. His bones, buried in Ravenna, witness against his countrymen: Florence, rejecting him alive, is denied him dead. This is poetic justice: the perfect contrapasso (Inferno 28.142). Eliot, on the other hand, freely renounced his US citizenship. We may infer from his adoption of British nationality and Anglican religion a repudiation of his family history since 1669, and his burial at East Coker as solidarity with his medieval ancestors.

Towards the end of his life, though Dante waxed nostalgic for the "sheepfold," that had nurtured him as a lamb (Paradiso 25.1-9), he did nothing to effect his return, adamantly feeling himself the aggrieved party, he felt Florence owed *him* an apology. He received it, posthumously, for he is pictured in their Duomo standing at her locked gates, offering the Divine Comedy to her glory. This, however, did nothing to lift the ban: his bones stayed in Ravenna and his tomb in the Church of Santa Croce remains an empty monument.

Eliot's exile revolved around a choice of vocation: either he would become a philosophy professor in the US or a poet in England. One could not write poetry in the US, for the poet requires the support of a culture. No such thing existed in US (at least, not since Andrew Jackson's election as president)! Returning to the US, he would have devoted himself to teaching at the expense of doing. He stayed in England and became a poet

Paradoxically, Eliot's repudiation of US citizenship strengthened his identification with this country. "An American poet," he pointed out, "writing in English does not write English poetry."[60] Moreover, in the 1950's Eliot, returned to St. Louis, admitted an unprecedented phenomenon: a single language giving birth to two literatures.[61] Perhaps, then, the US had a culture, after all, of which a literature was a manifestation? If so, then Eliot was, like St. Louis, set down at the confluence of two mighty rivers, an eminent witness to their joining.

*   *   *

Unless your ancestors were Asian, the American continent filled up right to left: the East Coast peopled from Europe and Africa with the leftward filtering of those who competition proven supernumerary, of late arrivals unable to find adequate seating or those unable to rest their itchy feet. Eliot's grandfather, The Rev. William Greenleaf Eliot, was of the latter type: in the 1830's he packed his household gods and ventured into the hinterland, a latter day Father Abraham. He was a Unitarian minister, his religion of a Kantian kind consisting of more imperatives than prohibitions, a religion that demanded the forsaking of self-seeking in the name of City, Church and University.[62]

In typical Eliot fashion, Grandfather Eliot built a home, a Church, a school for his daughters, a university where he could teach and performed so many other good works as to be tiresome to list, much less contemplate (Eliot's mother, herself a frustrated poet, authored a biography of her father-in-law to inspire her children). Dealing with such people one feels them spurred by the devil's hot breath on napes of their necks. They do not register it consciously, nor, if asked would they acknowledge it, but they are *driven*, not drawn.

These things, perhaps, skip a generation. Just as Eliot's grandfather left Massachusetts for the banks of the Mississippi, so he left the US for England. Paradoxically, by repudiating everything his grandfather stood for, Eliot became him.

*   *   *

Every Abraham needs an Isaac, a sacrificial lamb in residence. Eliot's father, Henry Ware Eliot, Sr., wanted to be a painter, but contented himself merely to disappoint his father's desire that he enter the ministry. His refusal was couched in vivid metaphor, "Too much pudding," he said, "choked the dog."[63] Father Eliot found his niche running a brickyard, feeding a growing town's hunger for real estate. This made his fortune and he built a home in the shadow of his father's. When his father died in 1887, his mother understandably wished to stay in the home her husband had built for her. Father Eliot and his family, stuck to the fly-paper of filial duty, remained in a decaying quarter of the city to be near his mother.

This is *not* to say they stayed in St. Louis the year round. Starting in 1893 (when young Tom was five), they began taking long annual vacations in New England (we may take this as Father Eliot's habitual halfway rebellion: a partial return from paternal exile), from June to October, first in New Hampshire, then Father Eliot, in 1896, built a summer home in Massachusetts on Gloucester Bay.

*   *   *

Some day I want to write an essay about the point of view of an American who wasn't an American, because he was born in the South and went to school in New England as a small boy with a nigger drawl, but who wasn't a southerner in the south because his people were northerners in a border state and looked down on all southerners and Virginians, and who so was never anything anywhere and who therefore felt himself to be more a Frenchman than an American and more an Englishman than a Frenchman and yet felt that the USA up to a hundred years ago was a family extension.[64]

This gypsy-life affected young Tom curiously. He was a Yankee in St. Louis and a Southerner in New England. He lost his Southern drawl without acquiring the Boston twang, just as later he would lose "his American accent without developing English speed and English slurring or English speech rhythms."[65] This oscillation of childhood winters and summers make their impression on The Dry Salvages in its dual first movement landscapes: one from St. Louis, the other from Massachusetts.

*   *   *

The Dry Salvages has been described as "the least successful poem of the series."[66] Some critics perhaps see in this an understatement:

At first sight it is not only incongruous with the others, strikingly different in conception and procedure, but different unaccountably and disastrously. One could take it by itself and prove convincingly that it is quite simply <u>rather a bad poem</u>.

It is hardly too much to say that the whole of the third quartet is spoken by a nameless persona; certainly it is spoken through a mask, <u>spoken in character</u>, spoken in character as the American.[67]

It is difficult to parry such cogent criticism, though I suspect the critic of hyperbole.[68] The Dry Salvages *is* different from the other Quartets, though I doubt "disastrously" so. And as one should never consider Purgatorio separately from Inferno and Paradiso (as its narrative has its beginning in one and end in the other), it, likewise, seems unfair to read The Dry Salvages in isolation from East Coker and Little Gidding. It is, moreover, odd to think of

The Dry Salvages as "spoken in character as the American" when the author *is* the American. Would it not make more sense to say the other poems are "spoken in the character of the European," that here Eliot lets the mask slip and shows his face? In any case, The Dry Salvages' paradoxes are sharper than the others, its devices, more overt; and its stars, of an American firmament.

*   *   *

In Amadeus, the Emperor Josef declared Mozart's music tiresome because he used "too many notes." Mozart's answer (that he had used neither more nor fewer notes than his subject required) begs the question: "What was his subject?" If we do not know what the artist attempts, our judgment skims the surface of criticism, gauging only our pleasure or displeasure with the work of art.

There is much about the world that cannot or should not be expressed pleasingly. My wife once told me she didn't find the middle movements of Mahler's Ninth Symphony at all beautiful. I answered that the maestro would have been pleased that she had taken his point. Beauty, in these movements, would mark aesthetic failure, a loss of *nerve*. But the fact she had rightly understood the composer did not help her to *like* the Symphony, the composer's success marked by her displeasure.

*   *   *

In what follows, I have accepted the notion that the Dry Salvages is a parody. If this thesis is correct, we must name its subject. Parody, a rhetorical device, is a means to an end. Bach, for instance, reused music he had written for secular occasions in his religious cantatas, making sacred the profane. For him, parody was akin to alchemy. I think The Dry Salvages parodies Walt Whitman's poem, Passage to India, and offers a corrective to Whitman's romanticized vision of Indic thought.

*   *   *

105

The Dry Salvages' status as the "American poem" was cemented when Eliot's British editor asked him:

A) Is "Dry Salvages" a place name?

B) What is a "groaner" (I.32)?[69]

Thus, definitions precede the poem:

(The Dry Salvages – presumably les trios sauvages – is a small group of rocks, with a beacon, off the N.E. coast of Cape Ann, Massachusetts. Salvages is pronounced to rhyme with assuages.

Groaner: a whistling buoy.)

Though the 'groaner' definition is self-explanatory, Eliot's etymology of the "Dry Salvages" is nonsense. By "les trios sauvages" (the three savages), he refers to the outcrop of rock in Gloucester Bay consisting of the Dry Salvages, the Little Salvages and the Flat Ground.[70] The Dry Salvages is "a bare ledge about fifteen feet above high water near the middle of a reef about 500 yards long in a northerly direction."[71] No documents attach the adjective "dry" to the rocks prior to 1867, when a derivation from 'trois' would be unlikely. "'Dry,'" moreover, "is not an unusual designation along the Atlantic coast for ledges bare at high water, to distinguish them from others which, like the Little Salvages, are covered twice daily."[72]

In contrast to the correlatives of the other poems, the Dry Salvages is not a place Eliot visited, but one he *avoided*. As Eliot described it:

And the ragged rock in the restless waters,
Waves wash over it, fogs conceal it;
On a halcyon day it is merely a monument,
In navigable weather it is always a seamark
To lay a course by: but in the sombre season
Or the sudden fury, is what it always was. (II.118-123)

It is, and always was, a menace to sailors rounding Cape Ann.

Movement No. 1

I do not know much about gods; but I think that the river
Is a strong brown god – sullen, untamed and intractable,

Patient to some degree, at first recognised as a frontier;
Useful, untrustworthy, as a conveyor of commerce;
Then only a problem confronting the builder of bridges.
The problem once solved, the brown god is almost forgotten
By the dwellers in cities — ever, however, implacable.
Keeping his seasons and rages, destroyer, reminder
Of what men choose to forget. Unhonoured, unpropitiated
By worshippers of the machine, but waiting, watching and waiting.
(I.1-10)

We ignore at our peril that the poem begins with a disclaimer: the critical voice, who calls the river a god, denies knowing what a god *is*, ironically espousing and rejecting paganism in a single breath. But why espouse paganism at all?

Seeing the river as a god recognizes His transcendence, His purposes and wisdom beyond our fathoming; His time, dwarfing human scale, outlasting families and nations, without imaginable beginning nor any end. We live in His world: not He in ours. He gives life and can take it: blessed be His name.

Eliot's rhetorical strategy in the first line espouses paganism in invidious comparison to modernity. Paganism was worshipful of the gods to a superstitious fault. Modernity forgets the gods, worshipping its own technological virtuosity. Paganism denounces this attitude as hubris and modernity's triumphs as "glittering vices."

*   *   *

At one season, it may move sluggishly in a channel so narrow that, encountering it for the first time at that point, one can hardly believe that it has travelled hundreds of miles, and has yet many hundreds of miles to go; at another season it may obliterate the low Illinois shore to a horizon of water, while in its bed it runs with a speed no man or beast can survive in it. At such times it carries down human bodies, cattle and houses.[73]

The river is time as it is experienced, as the flow of events our minds order by before and after, as the surge of blood bearing life through our bodies. As we number each day to sequence it within the cycles of the sun, so we give each event a

107

coordinate in time. Our inability to *return* to any prior time to prove memory and event coincide shows the system's ineffectuality. The past really *is* past, existing only in echoes and remnants, and a number cannot bring it back: time's "current" is too strong. History is rumor and opinion, perhaps informed opinion, but opinion none the less: that which would prove it fact is irretrievably lost, and with it the days of a human life.

*   *   *

Newtonian time was an objective abstraction, broken into identical units. Einstein's idea is nearer our experience. He explained relativity saying, "Put your hand on a hot stove for a minute and it will seem an hour. Talk to a pretty girl for an hour and it will seem a minute." Time, as experienced, is not a uniform flow of units of equal duration, but speeds up and slows down at the dictates of the contents of consciousness.

*   *   *

A river, a very big and powerful river, is the only natural force that can wholly determine the course of human peregrination. At sea, the wanderer may sail, or be carried by the winds and currents in one direction or another; a change of wind or tide may determine fortune. In the prairie, the direction of movement is more or less at the choice of the caravan; among mountains there will often be an alternative, a guess at the most likely pass. But the river with its strong, swift currents is the dictator to the raft or to the steamboat. It is a treacherous and capricious dictator.[74]

Eliot, in his preface to Huckleberry Finn, explains the river's power and with it, that of time. Dark Age monks rode rafts on the ocean's currents, allowing God to choose where they would land and whom they would serve. Eliot's grandparents, though not venturing so far as mountains or prairies, chose likely ways west in a wagon caravan. Twain, among the last generation of steamboat pilots, by patience rote and experience became the river's intimate and a safe warden of lives and cargo.

*   *   *

It is no surprise the advent of the railroad coincided with the season of war. As it displaced the steamboat as the dominant means of transportation, it tipped the national axis from North-South to East-West. The slave-holding South, being marginalized by disruptive innovation, tried to wrench free, but the river, a treacherous and capricious dictator, dashes on the rocks those who would go their own way.

Though Missouri, a border state, did not join the rebellion, she still found herself transformed in the minds of her countrymen: she, without moving an inch, changed regions from the Southwest to the Midwest. More ominously, the railroad threatened St. Louis. She, at the confluence of two mighty rivers (Mississippi and Missouri) had been an outlet for western goods to the South, but the railroad bypassed her, crossing the river at easier and safer fords. If she wanted the railroad, she must provide a bridge:

Belatedly the city engaged James Buchanan Eads to grapple with the river's fifteen-hundred-foot width; powerful scouring currents and winter ice jams; wide swings in volume between low water and flood stage; and a sixty foot change in the depth of bedrock. Eads spanned the "problem confronting the builders of bridges" by three upright ribbed arches of cast steel, each stretching over five hundred feet between piers sunk over one hundred feet through water and sand to rest on a sloping bedrock. When it opened July 4, 1874, the bridge was the largest ever built. Thus it entered St. Louis lore, an engineering and aesthetic masterpiece.[75]

The bridge accommodated rail and pedestrian traffic. Eliot recalled his childhood pleasure when taken to view the flooded river from the bridge. Thus, "the builder of bridges" "tamed" the river, turning the "strong brown god" into a spectacle for children.

*   *   *

As the bridge "corrected" geography, so, as Whitman points out, did the Suez Canal:

109

I see in one the Suez canal initiated, open'd,
I see the procession of steamships,
the Empress Engenie's leading the van,
I mark from on deck the strange landscape, the pure sky, the level sand
in the distance,
I pass swiftly the picturesque groups, the workmen gather'd,
The gigantic dredging machines. (Passage to India 3)

Whitman was transported, in prophetic imagination, to the opening of the Suez Canal. No need to sail west, following Columbus (who never arrived), nor to chase Vasco da Gama around the Cape of Good Hope, nor vainly seek with Hudson a Northwest Passage. Geography "corrected," we sail directly from Europe to India via a man-made channel. The world is made smaller as distance is overcome.

*   *   *

His rhythm was present in the nursery bedroom,
In the rank ailanthus of the April dooryard,
In the smell of grapes on the autumn table,
And the evening circle in the winter gaslight. (I.11-14)

If the dwellers of cities, having conquered the river, wish to forget Him, their prayers go unanswered. The gods do not relinquish power because humans "forget" Them. The river personifies Nature, whose hold humanity, short of suicide, cannot break. Human culture is not inborn but a second nature superimposed on the first. We begin life, as neither speakers of language nor users of technology, but as natural beings, little animals who must learn a language and culture. The river had us at hello.

Leaving the river, Tom heard Nature's heartbeat in the springtime bloom of the foul-smelling ailanthus tree, in the pungent odor of Concord grapes on the autumnal dinner table, and in the winter halo cast by that most technological of devices, the gaslight. In summer he meets Nature at the sea.

*   *   *

The river is within us, the sea is all about us;
The sea is the land's edge also, the granite
Into which it reaches, the beaches where it tosses
Its hints of earlier and other creation:
The starfish, the horseshoe crab, the whale's backbone;
The pools where it offers to our curiosity
The more delicate algae and the sea anemone.
It tosses up our losses, the torn seine,
The shattered lobsterpot, the broken oar
And the gear of foreign dead men. The sea has many voices,
Many gods and many voices.
The salt is on the briar rose,
The fog is in the fir trees. (I.15-26)

Line 15 transports us from the middle (Missouri) to the edge of the land (Massachusetts)., Eliot, unlike Huckleberry Finn does not ride the river south. His family took the train *east*. The river is forsaken as image of human time, to be replaced by the land.

In East Coker we saw the sea as time of a different order than the land. The land is human history, the succeeding of generations, the progress of science and evolving of the arts. The ocean surrounds human time with endless eons, with intimations of other creations, with the cold denial of human primacy or importance. The ocean stirs up from deep and elemental beds mementos of time before humanity. Things living, still alive, though from a time out of mind. Things dead, long dead, and evidences that once they lived. Things the sea found and discarded, lost by men the sea did not return. If the river is a god, the ocean is a pantheon.

*   *   *

Land and sea are figure and ground: you cannot simultaneously focus on both. The land is littered with the uses humans have had for Nature, of nations, cities, real estate and other human inventions. The ocean, graveyard from time immemorial, is limitless, trackless and huge beyond comprehending. Either we view the land from the sea, seeing

Nature conquered and distances overcome, or we anxiously look to the sea from land blurring humanity into insignificance.

*   *   *

There might be the experience of a child of ten, a small boy peering through sea-water in a rock-pool, and finding an sea-anemone for the first time: the simple experience (not so simple for the exceptional child as it looks) might lie dormant in his mind for twenty years, and re-appear transformed in some verse-context charged with great imaginative pressure.[76]

In the Charles Eliot Norton lectures at Harvard in 1932-33, Eliot, speaking nearly a decade before The Dry Salvages, calls his shot. Years later the dormant image *would* surface in a verse-context, making a poetic connection between the ocean, tossing up her hints of earlier and other creations and the poetic imagination, made in her image and likeness.

*   *   *

The sea howl
And the sea yelp, are different voices
Often together heard: the whine in the rigging,
The menace and caress of wave that breaks on water,
The distant rote in the granite teeth,
And the wailing warning from the approaching headland
Are all sea voices, and the heaving groaner
Rounded homewards, and the seagull:
And under the oppression of the silent fog
The tolling bell
Measures time not our time, rung by the unhurried
Ground swell, a time
Older than the time of chronometers, older
Than time counted by anxious worried women
Lying awake, calculating the future,
Trying to unweave, unwind, unravel
And piece together the past and the future,
Between midnight and dawn, when the past is all deception,

The future futureless, before the morning watch
When time stops and time is never ending;
And the ground swell, that is and was from the beginning,
Clangs
The bell. (I.26-48)

Eliot paints the ocean in a palette of sound. The fog-horn's insistent howl warns us not to rely on our eyes. We navigate by faith and not by sight. The sea gull yelps, searching for food. The wind whines running through the rigging. A wave kisses a hidden shoal with a smack that may be taken as admonition or siren's song. The rote, the roar of the ocean's endless collision with the land, is the deep, bass note grounding the polyphony. Entering the harbor warning surrounds us, for land and sea, in their embrace, are a greater menace than either alone.[77]

The tolling bell measures time, but not the crystalline Newtonian time of chronometers. Nor does it tally human history and succession. In East Coker, men and women whirled together around the fire. Here, women wait like Penelope, unweaving by night that they had woven by day, in clammy, midnight sweat retracting brave noontime affirmations, dreading a widowhood that would prove past happiness a suffering, a grief proving love a deceitful brook from which none draw water. The tolling bell measures time oblivious to human time, for the ocean sleeps in a cradle the moon rocks and the bell keeps the rhythm of her rocking.

Movement No. 2

J. Alfred Prufrock demurred to ask his "overwhelming question," substituting a different query:
And would it have been worth it, after all,
After the cups, the marmalade, the tea,
Among the porcelain, among the talk of you and me,
Would it have been worth while,
To have bitten off the matter with a smile,
To have squeezed the universe into a ball

113

> To roll it toward an overwhelming question,
> To say, "I am Lazarus, come from the dead,
> Come back to tell you all, I shall tell you all" –
> If one, settling a pillow by her head,
>> Should say: "That is not what I meant at all.
>> That is not it at all."

Love might have resurrected his heart as Lazarus from the tomb, but he, fearing he had misunderstood her actions, which he had taken for tokens of an answering affection, would not risk declaring himself lest she should disabuse him.

Eliot, as a young man, invented the middle-aged, ineffectual Prufrock. The middle-aged Eliot now asks the question Prufrock failed to utter. But nothing is as simple as that. As fear of rejection thwarted Prufrock, so Eliot must suffer trial to ask his question. Once again, the sensual voice cannot speak the soul directly, resorting to a formal periphrasis.

The rack of his torture is a rigid poetic form: the sestina. Sestinas are, typically, lover's laments, the poet lost in a cruel labyrinth of language. Arnaut Daniel is credited with its invention. Daniel was pointed out to Dante on the Terrace of the Lustful as "the best fashioner in the mother tongue of love songs and prose romances, surpassing all" (Purgatorio 26.117-119, Eliot, dedicating The Waste Land to Ezra Pound, quoted this passage). Dante wrote a double sestina to his beloved Beatrice, or, rather, to her grave. He was a lover trapped in his love, for love is as strong as death (Song of Songs 8.6).

*   *   *

Eliot adapted the sestina to his purposes. Sestinas are usually composed of six six-line stanzas the line endings of the first stanza repeated in the others, but scrambled chiastically so the ending of line 1 in stanza one ends line 2 in stanza two and the ending of line 6 in stanza one ends line 1 in stanza two, from there, the line endings alternate in stanza two, as 5,2,4,3. The pattern, repeated through six stanzas, ends with the rhyme scheme of stanza 1 turned inside-out. Eliot's innovation is the omission of the line switching: his sestina is dead, the lines endings monotonously motionless.

This is cited as evidence of depression and poetic exhaustion:[78] the sestina, instead of manifesting its wonted virtuosity as the poet turns himself inside-out, is reduced to a rhythm of tortured regularity. The critics, projecting their anger at having to run so claustrophobic a maze, *generously* excuse Eliot with a, "He didn't mean it, he's just depressed." But I suspect Eliot, taking an existing poetic device and modifying it for effect, is in *complete* control of his medium. It is, moreover, a failure of method to claim a poem defective because it *accomplished* the poet's aims.

*   *   *

Eliot's demolition of an established poetic form is a homage to Dante (not unlike Dante's homage to Daniel, whom he allowed to speak Provencal (Purgatorio 26.140-147) as Eliot will allow Dante to speak Italian (IV.177)). Eliot repeats on a small scale what Dante did in epic proportions.

Dante, unlike Milton, did not slavishly copy pagan conventions into his Christian Epic. Medieval Christianity *both* continued paganism and violently clashed with it, so Dante took measures both to preserve the classical epic and to *defile* it. He invented a new poetic form (terza rima), inscribing the Trinity into the fabric of his narrative. He wrote in rhyme, resorted to crude language and vernacular, transgressing classical decorum. Then, to crown to his efforts, he made the classical master Virgil his foil, allowing the readers to witness, at first hand, paganism's discomfort with the proceedings. But, above all, Dante made it a *Comedy* when the Classical Epic was tragic. We can only imagine Virgil's relief, when Beatrice brought the happy ending into view, to be returned to where the weather suited his clothes.

*   *   *

Where is there an end of it, the soundless wailing,
The silent withering of autumn flowers

115

Dropping their petals and remaining motionless;
Where is there an end to the drifting wreckage,
The prayer of the bone on the beach, the unprayable
Prayer at the calamitous annunciation?

There is no end, but addition: the trailing
Consequence of further days and hours,
While emotion takes to itself the emotionless
Years of living among the breakage
Of what was believed in as the most reliable —
And therefore the fittest for renunciation. (II.49-60)

The question is posed as a paradoxical speed bump: one, hurrying on, supposes that the "dropping of petals and remaining motionless" (physical death) should end the "soundless wailing," though it does not. In the words of the prophet:

"All flesh is grass, and all its beauty is like the flower of the field. The grass withers, the flower fades, when the breath of the LORD blows upon it; surely the people is grass." (Isaiah 40.6-7)

Eliot speaks not of the individual, but the human race who, continue the "soundless wailing" as generations replace each other. The "soundless wailing," implacable as a fog horn, announces not only death, but also a birth that *adds* to the wailing. This wailing is all the more poignant in a time of war with the sea roiled by drifting wreckage.

*   *   *

The prophet asked, "Is there no balm in Gilead? Is there no physician there?" (Jeremiah 8.22). A Negro spiritual answered, "There is a balm in Gilead." Obviously, in Eliot's opinion, they were just saying that to be nice. Answering his own question (Where is there an end of it, the soundless wailing?), he denies any end to it, only more of the same. A life, as it stretches out in time, only increases the deafening rote of the sea striking the land: death and life smashing into each other as relentlessly as the tide.

116

There is the final addition, the failing
Pride or resentment at failing powers,
The unattached devotion which might pass for devotionless,
In a drifting boat with a slow leakage,
The silent listening to the undeniable
Clamour of the bell of the last annunciation.

Where is the end of them, the fishermen sailing
Into the wind's tail, where the fog cowers?
We cannot think of a time that is oceanless
Or of an ocean not littered with wastage
Or of a future that is not liable
Like the past, to have no destination.

We have to think of them as forever bailing,
Setting and hauling, while the North East lowers
Over shallow banks unchanging and erosionless
Or drawing their money, drying sails at dockage;
Not as making a trip that will be unpayable
For a haul that will not bear examination. (II.61-78)

      As if the "calamitous annunciation" were not enough, we lack the good sense to curl our toes and die of pain and boredom. Old men should be explorers, but their boats slowly leak, but not so slowly they can keep up with the bailing. Their arms tire and, late or soon, give out. Who need ask for whom the bell tolls? And on land, others draw money making their fellows satisfied and comfortable – as their houses burn down around them.

*   *   *

      We die, not only as bodies, but also as a culture: the more we know the less it satisfies. Korean dance videos proliferate like kudzu, but the Word, neither bought nor sold, remains unspoken and unheard above the din of the last annunciation. When all discourse is commercial, it is, necessarily, paltry.

Death may set life's value, making each day a vanishing capital and adding new sins to the sinking fund of the race, but it cannot give life significance. Death, a hidden shoal, may cause hope to founder, but it cannot give life meaning. Eliot's question has the air of sea-sickness: what is the soundless wailing but the fore-knowledge of death? How can we live our lives in the shadow of our own tombstone?

An answer dispatched in East Coker is merging into a social role, becoming no more than an empty suit of clothes. Thus, gray hair, applied as an actor's makeup, denotes wisdom. Unlike the fishermen, pursuing sustenance in leaky boats, these keep safely to the shore hawking goods that will not survive eternity's inspection (1 Corinthians 3.10-15).

*   *   *

There is no end of it, the voiceless wailing,
No end to the withering of withered flowers,
To the movement of pain that is painless and motionless,
To the drift of the sea and the drifting wreckage,
The bone's prayer to Death its God. Only the hardly, barely prayable
Prayer of the one Annunciation. (II.79-84)

The overwhelming question (where is an end to it), answered negatively, would counsel despair but for the fact that only as human hope fades that a divine solution appears.

*   *   *

I was, perhaps, too hasty with the claim that Eliot disagreed with the slaves who sang of a "balm in Gilead." They perhaps illustrate his meaning most vividly as no one aspires to be a slave. Affirming life's goodness and one's own validity as a child of God despite the constant drum beat that one is less than human is the substance of the one Annunciation.

There can be no compromise or, rather, compromise is the siren's song of hidden shoal. We cannot escape death by living. Our only hope begins where human hope ends.

*   *   *

In the sixth month the angel Gabriel was sent from God to a city of Galilee named Nazareth, to a virgin betrothed to a man whose name was Joseph, of the house of David; and the virgin's name was Mary. And he came to her and said, "Hail, O favored one, the Lord is with you!" But she was greatly troubled at the saying, and considered in her mind what sort of greeting this might be. And the angel said to her, "Do not be afraid, Mary, for you have found favor with God. And behold, you will conceive in your womb and bear a son, and you shall call his name Jesus. He will be great, and will be called the Son of the Most High; and the Lord God will give to him the throne of his father David, and he will reign over the house of Jacob for ever; and of his kingdom there will be no end." And Mary said to the angel, "How shall this be, since I have no husband?" And the angel said to her, "The Holy Spirit will come upon you, and the power of the Most High will overshadow you; therefore the child to be born will be called holy, the Son of God. And behold, your kinswoman Elizabeth in her old age has also conceived a son; and this is the sixth month with her who was called barren. For with God nothing will be impossible." And Mary said, "Behold, I am the handmaid of the Lord; let it be to me according to your word." And the angel departed from her. (Luke 1.26-38)

The angel appeared to Mary, bringing news, not of glory, but of travail. She was a virgin, betrothed to Joseph. She was pregnant. What would she do? She surrendered, saying, "Behold, I am the handmaiden of the Lord." This is the one Annunciation.

But we, knowing the fetus in her womb is Jesus, are tempted overleap her anxiety, her fear of exposure for a sin she did not commit, her dread of Joseph's reaction when he finds out. We misunderstand: salvation is not in the outcome but her *surrender*.

We must not "cut to the chase," nor can we take the "darkness "as read." When solving the problem is at issue, the answer in the back of the book is useless. The Kingdom of Heaven differs from money which buys the same goods whether acquired by theft or labor. The Kingdom of Heaven and its means of acquisition are one and the same. The Kingdom of Heaven is not a what but a *how*.

*   *   *

The third movement of East Coker and this movement of The Dry Salvages parallel each other. The third movement of East Coker describes three darknesses (EC III.112-122):

1) The darkness of a theatrical change of scene (EC III.114-117)
2) The darkness of a stalled subway train (EC. 118-121)
3) The darkness of the patient under ether (EC III.122)

The darknesses and Annunciations correspond to each other, the first of the body, the second of the soul and the third of the spirit.

This parallelism is probably what Eliot means when he continues:

It seems, as one becomes older,
That the past has another pattern, and ceases to be a mere sequence —
Or even development: the latter a partial fallacy
Encouraged by superficial notions of evolution,
Which becomes, in the popular mind, a means of disowning the past.
(II.85-89)

Eliot originally continued, self-critically. "It seems, as one grows olderone has to repeat the same thing in a different way and risk being tedious." His editors found this remark an "embarrassing defensiveness," and Eliot cleaned it up.[79] He sees the three Annunciations as repetitions of the three darknesses. But he moved the argument forward by his focus on the modern desire to disown the past.

*   *   *

But 'tis a common proof,
That lowliness is young ambition's ladder,
Whereto the climber upward turns his face;
But when he once attained the upmost round,
He then unto the ladder turns his back,
Looks to the clouds, scorning the base degrees

By which he did ascend. (Julius Caesar Act I. scene 1)
        That's how Shakespeare put it. Power demands inevitability, the disowning a dubious past. Caesar was the luckiest general alive, but attributing power to luck only dares others to try theirs. Power is maintained by the help of Phoenician tales (Plato, Republic 3.414c), veiling Fortuna's pudenda under the cloak of inevitability.

*   *   *

        Caesar's son, to make his rule appear inevitable, hired a poet, Virgil, to write the foundation story of his house in the aftermath of the Trojan War. The ancients saw inevitability in an ancient lineage. The Jews rebelled against Rome three times before their religion was, finally, banned: the Romans so respected Jewish antiquity. The Christians needed no rebellion to provoke persecution: their recent origin proved their "religion" a superstition.

*   *   *

        Ovid traced the Roman view of time in his ages of Man (Metamorphoses 1.89-150). The world began in a golden age followed by ages of silver, bronze and the current iron age (the poet implicitly threatens us with ages of lead and tin). The pagans were conservative because they believed every step forward was also a step *down*. They could not use the words "new" and "improved" in the same sentence because they held "progress" and "deterioration" as synonyms.

*   *   *

        On the third day there was a marriage at Cana in Galilee, and the mother of Jesus was there; Jesus also was invited to the marriage, with his disciples. When the wine failed, the mother of Jesus said to him, "They have no wine." And Jesus said to her, "O woman, what have you to do with me? My hour has not yet come." His mother said to the servants, "Do whatever he tells you." Now six stone jars were

121

standing there, for the Jewish rites of purification, each holding twenty or thirty gallons. Jesus said to them, "Fill the jars with water." And they filled them up to the brim. He said to them, "Now draw some out, and take it to the steward of the feast." So they took it. When the steward of the feast tasted the water now become wine, and did not know where it came from (though the servants who had drawn the water knew), the steward of the feast called the bridegroom and said to him, "Every man serves the good wine first; and when men have drunk freely, then the poor wine; but you have kept the good wine until now." (John 2.1-10)

Imagine the paganism's amazement (expressed by the steward of the feast) as the bridegroom, unreasonably, withheld the choice wine until everyone was drunk on the cheap stuff. The notion of *development* entered the pagan world when Judaism and Christianity split into separate religions, the water of Jewish ablutions becoming Eucharistic wine.

Simultaneously, we gained a new way of thinking about time. Before Christianity, years were marked by the names of Consuls, time existing to perpetuate human fame. After, time became a countdown, a sequential numbering of years from the fullness of time to the end of the world. The pagans argued inconclusively whether the world had beginning or end. The Christians, sharing Jewish revelation's claimed the world had both, transforming time into a limited whole with both a starting point and a destination. Progress became conceivable.

*   *   *

The moments of happiness – not the sense of well-being,
Fruition, fulfilment, security or affection,
Or even a very good dinner, but the sudden illumination –
We had the experience but missed the meaning,
And approach to the meaning restores the experience
In a different form, beyond any meaning
We can assign to happiness. (II.90-96)

Time is change and we entered a timeless moment in the rose garden, but then words returned and took it from us. Time is change and everything I possess will cease, in time, to be mine.

That's what time is. But, by a shared logos, I may keep alive what I possess by sharing it with others. If my illumination begins and ends in me, it dims the moment sweet light no longer strikes my eyes. But if, by the logos, it is shared it ceases to be mine, becoming a common property. Thus, I insure myself against change by sharing that I had to lose.

*   *   *

I have said before
That the past experience revived in the meaning
Is not the experience of one life only
But of many generations — not forgetting
Something that is probably quite ineffable:
The backward look behind the assurance
Of recorded history, the backward half-look
Over the shoulder, towards the primitive terror. (II.96-103)

Eliot turns the corner from forgetting to remembrance (or, as he puts it, "not forgetting"). Modern forgetting gives us the appearance of inevitability. We are the outcome of a historical process, the ladder, once climbed, can be thrown away:[80] The primitive terror, having served its purpose as antecedent, is no longer of use. We thank God, like the Pharisees of old (Luke 18.10-14), that we are not like the pagans, worshipping idols in fear and trembling, forgetting that the substance of religious awe is that very fear and trembling.

*   *   *

If someone who lives in the midst of Christianity enters, with knowledge of the true idea of God, the house of God, the house of the true God, and prays, but prays in untruth, and if someone lives in an idolatrous land but prays with all the passion of infinity, although his eyes are resting upon the image of an idol – where, then, is there more truth? The one prays in truth to God although he is worshiping an idol; the other prays in untruth to the true God and is therefore in truth worshiping an idol.[81]

123

Progress does not abolish the human question. Whether hunter-gatherers or supermarket shoppers, human beings retain their primitive relation to food: we must eat to live. Likewise, religion, whatever its level of sophistication, is a passionate relation to a mystery that puts us to the question. False religion is a ready-made answer, not a question we answer with our lives. The primitive terror sculpts us into a shape the gods supply. Abolish the terror and reduce religion to ideology, the mind forged manacles of manipulation and control.

*   *   *

Now, we come to discover that the moments of agony
(Whether, or not, due to misunderstanding,
Having hoped for the wrong things or dreaded the wrong things,
Is not in question) are likewise permanent
With such permanence as time has. We appreciate this better
In the agony of others, nearly experienced,
Involving ourselves, than in our own.
For our own past is covered by the currents of action,
But the torment of others remains an experience
Unqualified, unworn by subsequent attrition.
People change, and smile: but the agony abides.
Time the destroyer is time the preserver,
Like the river with its cargo of dead negroes, cows and chicken coops,
The bitter apple, and the bite in the apple. (II.104-117)

We misunderstood the sudden illumination, thinking it would enhance our lives, and it does, but not in the way expected. We thought it would lead to joy, and it does, but only through travail. Our prayers are answered, but not as we had dreamed. We dreamt of glory, but are given an agony through which we pass into joy.

The suffering, the agony of life, the stuff of tragedy, has only the permanence of time. Time is change and when change ceases, agony ceases also. A prophet said to Mary:

"And a sword will pierce through your own soul also, that thoughts out of many hearts may be revealed." (Luke 2.35)

She did not understand until she stood at the foot of the Cross. The agony of life is not the end. The sword pierces our hearts to reveal what lies within and what it reveals is our salvation.

*   *   *

We see this more clearly in another's agony than our own. We are tales we tell ourselves and the good story is a pattern of cause and effect. We cover our past by the "currents of action," in our willful self-narration. We weave event and accident into "meaningful" patterns that prove us the central actor or victim in the agony of our lives.

Thus the necessity of "scriptural imagination,"[82] that means of telling a tale that by making it impersonal renders it personal. Consider, if you will, my servant Job, a blameless and upright man. His friends, seeing his suffering, turn it into opera, accusing him of a sin for which he is justly punished. He denies their accusations and the debate is on. They wrangle, chapter after chapter, while we, the readers, know, that Job's misfortune results, not from any sin, but from a bet taken far, far away. The argument, win or lose, is pointless.

We are told this about Job because we would not accept it told of ourselves. We are too powerful to believe in accidents. The author of Job lets us laugh at ourselves in the windy speeches of Job and his friends.

*   *   *

Time, paradoxically, is not only the destroyer, but also the preserver. This image grows in cogency when, in the next poem, it is applied to the refiner's or purgatorial fire, for here, the river of time does not refine, leaving behind only the detritus of time, decaying bodies washed ashore.

*   *   *

In autumn, the leaves fall,
        One after the other (until the branch sees

All its clothing spread on the ground),
So the evil seed of Adam's Fall
    Drop from that shore, one by one, (Inferno 3.112-116)

The bitter apple represents not only our anxiety in the face of death, but our guilt for our sins. We must not imagine the Fall as an historical event, as a debt Adam and Eve incurred that we must pay. Rather, it represents the simple truth that sin enters the world by a sin. Only by a first sin (of which Adam and Eve's provide the paradigm) do we each, in our turn, become sinners. Each individual human being is both herself and the race, and we each fall, one by one, into sin, taking our bite of the bitter apple.

*   *   *

And the ragged rock in the restless waters,
Waves wash over it, fogs conceal it;
On a halcyon day it is merely a monument,
In navigable weather it is always a seamark
To lay a course by: but in the sombre season
Or the sudden fury, is what it always was.

The ragged rock of sin bars us from our safe harbor. On a bright clear day, we cannot ignore it, remembering it as we cannot forget our deaths. In good weather, we can easily steer clear of it. When it is hidden by fogs of violent emotion that, in a somber season and sudden fury, remove us from ourselves, it makes of us a ship wreck.

Movement No. 3

I sometimes wonder if that is what Krishna meant –
Among other things – or one way of putting the same thing:
That the future is a faded song, a Royal Rose or a lavender spray
Of wistful regret for those who are not yet here to regret,
Pressed between yellow leaves of a book that has never been opened.
(III.124-127)

What did Krishna mean? The central issue in the Bhagavad Gita is incarnation (*avatarana*), though the Hindus differ from the Christians in not using the term in a historical sense. For Christians incarnation means God's one time only entry into the world of flesh and the senses. Lord Krishna, on the other hand, enters the world as often as needed ("Whenever right declines and wrong prevails, then, O Bharata, I come to birth." (Bhagavad Gita 4.7)). In the Bhagavad Gita, he is Arjuna's chauffer who, having driven him to the field of battle, harangues him on his duty.

*   *   *

Incarnation, Christian or Hindu, claims that, contrary to reason, the meaning of the world can be present in the world without being reduced to a fact *about* the world. This claim is an apparent contradiction because anything *in* the world is as it is accidentally as any true fact can be falsified without changing the world as a whole. If the meaning of the world were *in* the world it could be different than it is, but if the meaning of the world can change, the world has no meaning.[83] This, put in Christian terms, is the Good Friday paradox: If God is necessary Being, how can God die (pass out of being) and still be God?

Religions typically sidestep this apparent contradiction by the claim that the meaning of the world is not something *in* or *about* the world, but a *way* of being in the world that opens a vision transcending appearances (e.g. John 1.51). The "meaning" of the world is a *verb*, not a noun.

*   *   *

Eliot, questioning Lord Krishna's meaning, once again, makes a disclaimer. Just as he, calling the river a god, took it back with the counter-claim that he does not know what a god is (I.1), he does not offer his reading of Krishna's meaning without first admitting that he does not *know* what Krishna meant. Hinduism describes the journey of the soul, through many lives and identities, until it attains birthlessness (nirvana). Then it rests, knowing not God, but being God. Christianity describes the arrival of the only-begotten Son (monogenes (John 1.18)), who in word, deed and sacrificial death opened the path of salvation to all who receive his life-giving word, the Holy Spirit. These are incompatible visions and Eliot, from his Western, Christian perspective, refuses to claim to know what Krishna *really* meant, though he hazards to guess.

*   *   *

Regret? How do you regret the future, regret those as yet unborn? The past is indeed a faded song, its echo ever retreating, but the future, does it not rush *towards* us? Certainly, it seems so, but does it ever *arrive*? Just as the past is ever in retreat, so the future is ever advancing. Just as we may regret what we have done or left undone, so too we may "regret" the evil to which today is antecedent.

We call "regret," extended into the future, anxiety. The future, yet to come, impinges on the present with a foreboding of loss. We wager our souls on a roll of the dice, not knowing how they will come down. We project ourselves into the future, knowing and not knowing what awaits us. We know that death awaits us, but the rest is silence. How odd, then, that death, so often named the "final mystery" is all the future we really know.

*   *   *

Eliot's "backward half-look" at his youth and childhood brings us to his college years:

Two years spent in the study of Sanskrit under Charles Lanman, and a year in the mazes of Patanjali's metaphysics under the guidance of James Woods, left me in a state of enlightened mystification. A good half of the effort of understanding what the Indian philosophers were after – and their subtleties make most of the great European philosophers look like schoolboys – lay in trying to erase from my mind all the categories and kinds of distinction common to European philosophy from the time of the Greeks. My previous and concomitant study of European philosophy was hardly better than an

128

*obstacle. And I came to the conclusion – seeing also that the 'influence'
of Brahmin and Buddhist thought upon Europe, as in Schopenhauer,
Hartmann, Deussen, had largely been through romantic
misunderstanding – that my only hope of really penetrating to the
heart of the mystery would lie in forgetting how to think and feel as an
American or a European: which, for practical as well as sentimental
reasons, I did not wish to do.*[84]

That this is the next logical step in Eliot's autobiography does
not stop critics suggesting that "to introduce Krishna at this
point is an error and destroys the poem's imaginative
harmony."[85] If so, it is an obvious "error" (not unlike a dead
sestina), calling attention to itself, especially when preceded by
three prior references to the annunciation and immediately
followed by a prayer to the Virgin.

*   *   *

*If all men know God how can Paul say that the Galatians did
not know God prior to the hearing of the Gospel? I answer: There is a
twofold knowledge of God, general and particular. All men have the
general and instinctive recognition that there is a God who created
heaven and earth, who is just and holy, and who punishes the wicked.
How God feels about us, what His intentions are, what He will do for
us, or how He will save us, that men cannot know instinctively. It
must be revealed to them. I may know a person by sight, and still not
know him, because I do not know how he feels about me. Men know
instinctively that there is a God. But what His will is toward them,
they do not know.*[86]

Martin Luther explains the theological notion of the
duplex knowledge of God. In Eliot's parlance, the doctrine of a
religion (particular knowledge) is a superstructure built on the
foundation of universal wisdom (general knowledge). This is
best illustrated in a passage from the New Testament:
*Now when Jesus was born in Bethlehem of Judea in the days of Herod
the king, behold, wise men from the East came to Jerusalem, saying,
"Where is he who has been born king of the Jews? For we have seen his
star in the East, and have come to worship him." When Herod the king
heard this, he was troubled, and all Jerusalem with him; and*

assembling all the chief priests and scribes of the people, he inquired of them where the Christ was to be born. They told him, "In Bethlehem of Judea; for so it is written by the prophet: 'And you, O Bethlehem, in the land of Judah, are by no means least among the rulers of Judah; for from you shall come a ruler who will govern my people Israel.'" Then Herod summoned the wise men secretly and ascertained from them what time the star appeared; and he sent them to Bethlehem, saying, "Go and search diligently for the child, and when you have found him bring me word, that I too may come and worship him." When they had heard the king they went their way; and lo, the star which they had seen in the East went before them, till it came to rest over the place where the child was. When they saw the star, they rejoiced exceedingly with great joy; and going into the house they saw the child with Mary his mother, and they fell down and worshiped him. Then, opening their treasures, they offered him gifts, gold and frankincense and myrrh. And being warned in a dream not to return to Herod, they departed to their own country by another way. (Matthew 2.1-12)

The Magi, having only general knowledge (astrology), see signs in the heavens portending a great Jewish King. They reasonably expect to find this new-born King in the palace at Jerusalem. Their arrival sparks Herod's angst: there are no new-borns in his harem. He summons his scribes and they, having access to particular knowledge (revelation), quote the prophet:

But you, O Bethlehem Ephrathah, who are little to be among the clans of Judah, from you shall come forth for me one who is to be ruler in Israel, whose origin is from of old, from ancient days. (Micah 5.2)

that the sought-after babe is to be found in Bethlehem, enabling Herod to direct the Magi. The Magi, aware of the prophecies, begin, themselves, to participate in particular knowledge, finding the child by following a "star" and warned, in dreams, not to return to Herod.

*   *   *

Some readers, attracted by the occult, think only Asiatic literature has religious understanding. Others distrust mysticism and stay narrowly Christian. For both it is salutary to learn that the truth is not occult, and that it is not wholly confined on the one hand to their own religious tradition, or on the other hand to an alien culture and religion which they regard with superstitious awe.[87]

Eliot, versed in both Western and Eastern philosophy (though, himself, an Anglican convert), reinforces the claims of general knowledge before proceeding to particular knowledge. As the Four Quartets is not a specifically Christian poem, the Dry Salvages can begin in a mock espousal of paganism. It can also, in approaching particular knowledge, resort to Hindu, rather than Christian, scripture. While both scriptures advance differing claims (that is, in their particulars, are contradictory), neither conflict with general knowledge.

Eliot subtly argues against the claims of modern humanism. Humanism argues that as religious traditions disagree in their particulars, either one of them is right and all others are wrong, or none are right. If only one is right, then, religion seems arbitrary: better to be skeptical of all religions when salvation is the outcome of a lucky guess. Thus skepticism seems better than religion because it partakes of uncontroversial general knowledge, eschewing contradictory particular knowledge. This argument, to use an analogy, is like preferring to live in a cave to a finished house because architects disagree on how to configure the rooms.

*　　*　　*

A people that still believes in itself retains its own god. In him it reveres the conditions which let it prevail, its virtues: it projects its pleasure in itself, its feeling of power, into a being to whom one may offer thanks. Whoever is rich wants to give of his riches; a proud people needs a god: it wants to sacrifice.[88]

Nietzsche, often maligned as an atheist (the "God is dead" thing has been misunderstood), was actually a pagan who had no problem with gods, so long as they were made in the *human* image and likeness. How dare the Jewish God refuse to be so used! A true religion differs from paganism in that paganism sees its gods as larger, more powerful, more beautiful projections of ourselves, while a religion sees its God as a transcendence calling a people to overcome the human and become God-like.

*   *   *

Practically, it is hardly likely that even so great a poet as Dante could have composed the Comedy merely with understanding and without belief; but his private belief becomes a different thing in becoming poetry. It is interesting to hazard the suggestion that this is truer of Dante than of any other philosophical poet. With Goethe, for instance, I often feel too acutely "this is what Goethe the man believed," instead of merely entering into a world which Goethe has created; with Lucretius also; less with the Bhagavad Gita, which is the next greatest philosophical poem to the Divine Comedy within my experience. That is the advantage of a coherent traditional system of dogma and morals like the Catholic: it stands apart, for understanding and assent even without belief, from the single individual who propounds it.[89]

Goethe advocates a world-view he has come to, while Dante inherited Christianity whole. He is even uncomfortable with parts of it (for instance, its attitude towards homosexuality), but he was not given a choice and compromise is not an option (or, rather, his Inferno is the home of the compromiser). Likewise, the author of the Bhagavad Gita also expounds a doctrine not personally arrived at, but the expression of a *tradition*.

Eliot does neither. He is an orthodox Anglo-Catholic, but, for the purposes of this poem, he is an *explorer*, sailing the seas in a leaking boat. And, in his poem, we go with him.

*   *   *

Krishna, after a failed attempt to broker a peace, brought the warrior, Arjuna, to the field of battle, known as both the field of *dharma* (righteousness, virtue, duty) and the field of Kuru (land held by clan Kuru), the intersection of earthly striving and religious devotion. Arjuna surveys the enemy and sees among them many of his kinsmen and benefactors. He knows his cause is just, but doubts his right to slay those he owes debts of blood and loyalty, even though he is duty bound to do so. He resolves not to fight, but Lord Krishna talks him out of it, explaining how to proceed piously.

Krishna reminds Arjuna that his anxiety over killing kinsmen and benefactors springs from misidentifying them with their bodies and not with *Atman* (what a Christian might be tempted to call their immortal souls). The body may be killed, but not *Atman*, which simply clothes itself in new bodies when old ones are spent.

Then he argues, like Chaucer's Parson, "If gold rusts then what can iron do?" If Arjuna shirks battle, lesser men will not be edified by his noble motives, but impute to him the cowardice they recognize in themselves (this they call their "shrewdness"). They will be deprived of an example that might have taught them by confirming them in their ignorance.

He reminds Arjuna of each person's obligation to sacrifice to God, but he speaks, neither of the blood of bulls nor of goats, the practitioner of karma yoga offers God his *future*. The hypocrite sacrifices to God in hope of receiving again that he offers. The yogi sacrifices without expecting reward: he does right because it is right, eschewing the fruit of action. Thus Arjuna should go and kill with an "even-mind," completely unconcerned with the consequences of his actions, offering the dead to God as a sacrifice.

*   *   *

Gandhi wrote in the preface to his translation of the Bhagavad Gita:

When I first became acquainted with the Gita, I felt that it was not a historical work, but that, under the guise of physical warfare, it described the duel that perpetually went on in the hearts of mankind, and that physical warfare was brought in merely to make the description of the internal duel more alluring. This preliminary intuition became more confirmed on a closer study of religion and the Gita. A study of the Mahabharata‡ gave it added confirmation. I do not

---

‡ The Mahabharata is the epic of which Bhagavad Gita is part.

regard the Mahabharata as a historical work in the accepted sense. By ascribing to the chief actors superhuman or subhuman origins, the great Vyasa [author of the Mahabharata] made short work of the history of kings and their peoples. The persons therein described may be historical, but the author of the Mahabharata has used them merely to drive home his religious theme.[90]

Gandhi translated the Gita into the Gujarati dialect to offer it to a huge Hindu readership unversed in Sanskrit.

He, of course, faced a formidable challenge. Who can question his powerful motive to assert that, overt details aside, the Bhagavad Gita is <u>not</u> an incitement to war? Certainly, the poem begins with armies arrayed and Arjuna's despair at the prospect of killing so many relations and benefactors. And yes, as he is about to lay down his arms, Lord Krishna talks him out of it, causing his return to the fray with renewed resolve. And, moreover, it is Hindu scripture and Gandhi, as a Hindu, would greatly desire to "neutralize" a message contradicting his commitment to non-violence.

That being said, it would take a powerful misreading of the text to contradict Gandhi. One would have to explain why an exhortation to war contains material about rebirth, karma, duty and right-willing and nothing about worldly glory and the victor's right to spoils. It would be like interpreting the Book of Job as an explanation of how to regain a lost fortune.[91] Paradoxically, Gandhi's interested interpretation coincides with a disinterested view.

*   *   *

And the way up is the way down, the way forward is the way back.
You cannot face it steadily, but this thing is sure,
That time is no healer: the patient is no longer here. (III.129-131)

Heraclitus returns and in his voice Krishna speaks: to die is to be reborn, to be reborn is to die. The way up is the way down because life and death is a turning wheel. The patient is no longer here, not because he is dead, but at rest at the still point of the turning world.

*　　*　　*

Singing my days,
Singing the great achievements of the present,
Singing the strong light works of engineers,
Our modern wonders, (the antique ponderous Seven outvied,)
In the Old World the east the Suez canal,
The New by its mighty railroad spann'd,
The seas inlaid with eloquent gentle wires;
Yet first to sound, and ever sound, the cry with thee O soul,
The Past! the Past! the Past!

The Past — the dark unfathom'd retrospect!
The teeming gulf — the sleepers and the shadows!
The past — the infinite greatness of the past!
For what is the present after all but a growth out of the past?
As a projectile form'd, impell'd, passing a certain line, still keeps on, So
the present, utterly form'd, impell'd by the past. (Passage to India 1)

Whitman's poem, Passage to India, describes the conquest of space and its consequences. He cites as evidence three modern wonders: the Suez Canal, the transcontinental railroad and the transatlantic cable. These three "out vie" the ponderous seven ancient wonders, because they trumpet, not the pride or power of a single people or city, but link the world together, making the human race a single people.
Passage to India! Lo, soul, seest thou not God's purpose from the first?
 The earth to be spann'd, connected by network,
The races, neighbors, to marry and be given marriage,
The oceans to be cross'd, the distant brought near,
The lands to be welded together.

A worship new I sing, You captains, voyagers, explorers, yours,
You engineers, you architects, machinists, yours,
You, not for trade or transportation only,
But in God's name, and for thy sake O soul. (Passage to India 2)

Dante met, among the frauds in his Inferno, Ulysses who, like Columbus, made the "mad flight" west to a place thought "unpeopled" (Inferno 26.112-120). His "madness" was the

135

presumptuous hubris of transgressing limits set by the gods (the pillars of Hercules) in the pursuit of personal knowledge. Here, Whitman reverses Dante's judgment in the name of a new Avatar who will proclaim a single religion for a single human race. The captains, voyagers and explorers are not guilty of hubris, but have fulfilled God's initial purpose.

*   *   *

I see over my own continent the Pacific railroad surmounting every barrier,
I see continual trains of cars winding along the Platte carrying freight and passengers,
I hear the locomotives rushing and roaring, and the shrill steam-whistle,
 I hear the echoes reverberate through the grandest scenery in the world,
I cross the Laramie plains, I note the rocks in grotesque shapes, the buttes,
I see the plentiful larkspur and wild onions, the barren, colorless, sage-deserts,
I see in glimpses afar or towering immediately above me the great mountains, I see the Wind river and the Wahsatch mountains,
I see the Monument mountain and the Eagle's Nest, I pass the Promontory, I ascend the Nevadas,
I scan the noble Elk mountain and wind around its base,
I see the Humboldt range, I thread the valley and cross the river,
I see the clear waters of lake Tahoe, I see forests of majestic pines,
Or crossing the great desert, the alkaline plains, I behold enchanting mirages of waters and meadows,
 Marking through these and after all, in duplicate slender lines,
Bridging the three or four thousand miles of land travel,
Tying the Eastern to the Western sea,
The road between Europe and Asia. (Passage to India 3)

Whitman calls to mind a visionary landscape: the transcontintental railroad, tying together oceans. He celebrates the conquest of space and the first era of globalization that would end in the first Great War: the world would not be so mobile again until the fall of the Iron Curtain. Less than a century later, Eliot's train passengers would see it all differently:

When the train starts, and the passengers are settled
To fruit, periodicals and business letters
(And those who saw them off have left the platform)
Their faces relax from grief into relief,
To the sleepy rhythm of a hundred hours.
Fare forward, travellers! not escaping from the past
Into different lives, or into any future;
You are not the same people who left that station
Or who will arrive at any terminus,
While the narrowing rails slide together behind you; (III.132-141)

The days of World War II were, in England especially, no place for grandiose dreams of messiahs. Or rather, they were, but the British, wanting no part of Hitler were doggedly fighting the dream. The fight was as yet undecided, but, if the rest of Europe was any indication, the outcome would be tears. But, as Arjuna illustrates, if you focus on the fruit of action you lose your resolve.

Focus on the outcome and anxiety eats the sinew of the soul. We must focus on the day immediately before us. No looking out on grand vistas: we cannot afford to take our eye off the ball. Eliot's small and intensely local landscapes clash with Whitman's expansive vistas. Instead of the conquest of space Eliot's train represents the vehicle of karma: the people who embark will not be those who disembark. Heraclitus' voice merges with Krishna's: we remain the same, not in spite of change, but because of it.

*   *   *

If the good or bad exercise of the will does alter the world, it can alter only the limits of the world, not the facts — not what can be expressed by means of language.

In short the effect must be that it becomes an altogether different world. It must, so to speak, wax and wane as a whole.

The world of the happy man is a different one from that of the unhappy man.[92]

The penitent is never the person who sinned, for repentance has reshaped her world: she remembers in pain an act that once gave her pleasure. True penitence regrets, not the *outcome* of the action, but the action itself, regardless whether it resulted in failure or fortune. Thus the penitent differs from the sinner, for the penitent will not sin again, even if sinner and penitent are the "same" person.

*   *   *

And on the deck of the drumming liner
Watching the furrow that widens behind you,
You shall not think 'the past is finished'
Or 'the future is before us'.
At nightfall, in the rigging and the aerial,
Is a voice descanting (though not to the ear,
The murmuring shell of time, and not in any language)
'Fare forward, you who think that you are voyaging;
You are not those who saw the harbour
Receding, or those who will disembark.
Here between the hither and the farther shore
While time is withdrawn, consider the future
And the past with an equal mind. (III.142-154)

The last of Whitman's three modern wonders (the seas inlaid with eloquent gentle wires) is replaced by the rigging and the aerial (the wireless). Instead of a code of dots and dashes, a "voice" descants from the murmuring shell of time. Here, technology, with its hope of a new revelation, is banished by the voice of the eternal sea.

By a pun, Eliot connects modern technology and the elemental spirit of Shakespeare's romance, The Tempest.[93] And this, further connects to the annunciation as Gabriel is ministering spirit to Mary, as Ariel is to Prospero. But note that Eliot's usage describes no a triumph over nature, but, as in Dante's Paradiso, a condescension: the voice of God mediated to us in a transcendental "language."

*   *   *

Emily's time in the rose garden with Eliot had cost her. She did not get back to California before her employer had given her job to another. He had taken a chance on her despite her lack of a college degree and such employers were few. This left Emily destitute, living in Boston with her unstable mother and deeply depressed.

Eliot, separated from Vivienne, had taken steps to keep out of her sight (including moving into a spare room in a rectory above a tube station). This, of course, meant that she was avid to see him. She stalked him, turning Eliot's life into an endless game of "Tag, you're it." Emily's depression became just the ticket to put an ocean between himself and his tormentor. He got on a boat to America.

In the time taken to think on the drumming liner, between the hither and the farther shore, while time was withdrawn, he could not imagine Vivienne (the past) was finished. On leaving the boat he considered the future (Emily) with an equal mind.

On seeing Emily he was appalled, he could not imagine so profound a depression not leaving a scar (so to speak) on her soul (that is, *if* she recovered). His presence in Boston, while palliative, did nothing to actually help Emily. Though, he could not employ Emily, he *could* take the job on offer on the faculty at Harvard, divorce Vivienne, marry Emily and pray Vivienne could not get a passport. But, having separated from one mad wife, could he be expected to divorce her and take up with another? Considering the future (Emily) with an even mind, he got on a boat and returned to England.

The parody is a consequence of reading Eliot's ideal of even-mindedness in splendid isolation, as if an individual could, of himself, attain to it. Eliot is too often read in this way, and such reading is nothing less than a mockery.

*   *   *

Eliot's editor, on reading the command, "Fare forward" asked whether it was from Browning. Eliot answered, cagily,

'"Fare forward." I had quite forgotten the Browning, and I don't even remember it now. I was thinking of the words of the sibyl to Alaric (wasn't it) on his way to Rome: not fare well but fare forward."[94]

Actually the reference is to "Murder in the Cathedral" and is spoken to Thomas Becket by his final tempter:

Fare forward to the end.
All other ways are closed to you
Except the way already chosen,
But what is pleasure, kingly rule,
Or the rule of men beneath king,
With craft in corners, stealthy stratagem,
To the general grasp of spiritual power?[95]

The final temptation is to martyrdom, the temptation to which Mary of Scots succumbed, saying, "In my end is my beginning." Beckett is tempted to martyrdom as a usurper seizes the throne making *himself* king. But the saint, very different from a king, operates under a different code. The king, in compassing the crown, takes to himself the fruit of action. The saint, in giving his life, offers himself for *others*: the fruit of his sacrifice enriching them. Thomas dies not for his own glory, but to take away the peoples' fear, leaving them an example of brave resistance.

Shakespeare wrote no play about Beckett because the Tudors, absolute monarchs, hated him and did all in their power to suppress his pilgrimage. Likewise, Murder in the Cathedral was popular during the war years as an incitement to stand against Hitler.

*   *   *

At the moment which is not of action or inaction
You can receive this: "on whatever sphere of being
The mind of a man may be intent
At the time of death" — that is the one action
(And the time of death is every moment)
Which shall fructify in the lives of others:
And do not think of the fruit of action.
Fare forward.
O voyagers, O seamen,

You who came to port, and you whose bodies
Will suffer the trial and judgement of the sea,
Or whatever event, this is your real destination.'
So Krishna, as when he admonished Arjuna
On the field of battle.
Not fare well,
But fare forward, voyagers. (III.155-182)

Lord Krishna said:

Action alone is the province, never the fruits thereof. Let not thy motive be the fruit of action, nor shouldst thou desire to avoid action. Act thou, O Dhananjaya, without attachment, steadfast in yoga, even-minded in success and failure. Even-mindedness is yoga. Work without attachment, being established firmly in yoga. (Bhagavad Gita 2.47-48)[96]

Arjuna, the warrior, is to offer himself as a sacrifice in the time of war. He is not to judge consequences, but to perform his socially mandated task as an example to lesser men. The fruits of action are offered to the god, we must not take them, lest we become thieves. Nor, if we pursue the fruit of action, can we act with an even-mind, for then, we must do what we must to attain the fruit and not what we should. This is Eliot's counsel to England in the time of war.

*   *   *

Lord Krishna said:

Or whatever form a man continually contemplates, that same he remembers in the hour of death, and to that very form he goes, O Kaunteya. (Bhagavad Gita 8.6)[97]

Eliot, taking this verse into his poem, makes an accommodation:

Sinha points out that Krishna's words in the Gita are usually interpreted as "The mind of man as it is at the time of death is fructified in the next life of that man, i.e. in rebirth." Eliot omits the reference to rebirth and has the moment fructify "in the lives of others."[98]

The compromise with Christianity is clear:

141

I am the vine, you are the branches. He who abides in me, and I in him, he it is that bears much fruit, for apart from me you can do nothing. (John 15.5)

This speech occurs as Jesus promulgates his second commandment:

"This is my commandment, that you love one another as I have loved you. Greater love has no man than this, that a man lay down his life for his friends. You are my friends if you do what I command you." (John 15.12-14)

Christianity, being historical, lacks any idea of karma, though it is steeped in self-sacrifice. Eliot, quoting the terms of karma yoga, adapts them to a Christian context in speaking to a Christian nation at war.

Movement No. 4

Lady, whose shrine stands on the promontory,
Pray for all those who are in ships, those
Whose business has to do with fish, and
Those concerned with every lawful traffic
And those who conduct them.

Repeat a prayer also on behalf of
Women who have seen their sons or husbands
Setting forth, and not returning:
Figlia del tuo figlio,
Queen of Heaven. (IV.169-178)

Eliot's elegiac prayer to the Lady seems a petition for those lost at sea, but, at a deeper level, iy is a specific instance of a universal. As Mary, from the foot of the Cross, images mortal loss of every shape or size, so the lost seamen represent all who have entered eternity. The prayer to the Virgin, though jerking us from Bhagavad Gita to the Paradiso, advances the logic of the poem, by faring us forward" at the cost of our lives: the most precious is the most worthy of renunciation (II.59-60). Eliot, in his prayer, laments national grief and anxiety (regret for the lost and anxiety for what will be lost) in the war.

142

*   *   *

Dante's Comedy consists of 100 songs (cantos) divided into three song-cycles (canticles), one for each realm of the afterlife: 33 cantos for Purgatory and Paradise and Inferno, transgressing the pattern, with 34. It tells the tale of a woman sent from Heaven on a mission to save her reprobate lover who is mindlessly en route to perdition. She descends to the Earth and through it up the cone of Hell. In the highest circle of Hell she enlists the aid of one she is sure her lover will heed: the poet Virgil. Then she is off, returning through Hell, to await his deliverance. Thus began Dante's time with Virgil which ended with Dante and Beatrice reunited in the Garden of Eden, his innocence restored.

This is not the end of Beatrice's providence. She guides Dante through the nine lower Heavens, through planets and stars, until they arrive in the highest heaven, beyond time and space. Then, she is gone. She did not abandon him. It is only here that the extent of her care becomes fully evident: the goal of Dante's journey is an audience with God. But God is not approached unbidden: an appointment is necessary. The receptionist is the Mother of God. Beatrice, having thought of everything, had prevailed upon one of Her favorites, St. Bernard of Clairveaux, to succeed her as Dante's final guide. If Bernard can't pray Dante past the Virgin nobody can.

*   *   *

Bernard prays:
"Virgin Mother, daughter of your Son
Humbler and higher than any creature,
Fixed end of the Eternal Plan.
You granted to human nature
Such nobility that its Creator
Did not scorn to make Himself a creature.
Within your womb that Love rekindled
Whose warmth – in eternal peace –

Brought this flower to blossom.
For us here you are the noonday torch of charity
      And below, among mortals,
      The living fountain of eternal hope.
Lady, you are so high, and so prevail
      That he who seeks grace, but not your aid
      Would have his wish, wingless, fly.
Your loving kindness succors not only
      Those who ask, but oft times
      Freely gives before the asking.
In you is mercy, in you, compassion,
      In you, magnificence -- in you unite
      Whatever good is found in any creature.
This man who from the deepest pit
      In the universe up to this height
      Has seen, one by one, the lives of spirits,
Now pleads that you grant by your grace
      The power to raise his eyes higher still
      That he may rise to the ultimate salvation.
And I, who have never burned for my own vision
      More than I burn for his, offer all my prayers
      Praying that they will suffice --
That you disperse, by your prayer,
      Every cloud of mortality that the
      Highest joy may unfold before him.
I pray you also, O Queen, who can do
      What she wills, keep his affection pure
      After his vision and when he returns.
Guard him against his mortal urges:
      See that Beatrice, and all the blest
      Join me in my prayer, folding their hands to you." (Paradiso
33.1-39)

Before Bernard finishes speaking, Dante is already ascending to God.

*   *   *

The prayers connect at line IV.177, a direct quotation of the Italian of Paradiso 33.1. Robert Frost said poetry's music is lost in translation. The translation "daughter of your Son" (in that she, though the Mother of God, as a Christian, *inherits* her throne from her son) transfers the sense of "Figlia del tuo figlio" at the cost of its music.

*   *   *

After the war, Ezra Pound received a postcard from a friend in the States (Possum, as in Old Possum's Book of Practical Cats, is an Eliot nom de plume):

Dear E. P. et famille:
Here is my Lady that Possum stole. Best Dead Madonna this side of the Atlantic . . . .
Yrs. Olson

The postcard pictured the Church of Our Lady of Good Voyage in Gloucester, Massachusetts, crowned with a statue of Our Lady bearing a fishing boat instead of the infant Jesus on her left arm. Eliot's response was emphatic:

Mr. Olson or Olsen is in error. I have never returned to Cape Ann or Gloucester Mass since 1915. Presumably this statue tops the façade of the R.C. Church in Gloucester. I do not think it was there in my time: anyway I had no knowledge of its existence when I wrote 'The Dry Salvages.' But I thought there <u>ought</u> to be a shrine to the B.V.M. at the harbor mouth of a fishing port. The Church on which this statue stands is probably in the town itself. T.S.E. 14.8.47[99]

Eliot was right that the Church *is* in the town, but the statue topped it only much later.[100] But if you think he is merely being contrary:

When, in 1961, the Rev. William T. Levy mentioned to Eliot his admiration for the Church of Notre Dame de la Gard, high up overlooking the Mediterranean Sea at Marseilles, Eliot told him that this was the 'shrine' he had in mind. He reports Eliot as saying, in response to his expressing surprise at not having realized this:
"You accepted it as a class of churches, and were not thinking of a particular church. And that is the right way to think of it. It is fortuitous in our case that I as writer and you as reader of these lines happened to know and react identically to the same place – and then we had to know each other for me to affirm it."[101]

145

Also pray for those who were in ships, and
Ended their voyage on the sand, in the sea's lips
Or in the dark throat which will not reject them
Or wherever cannot reach them the sound of the sea bell's
Perpetual angelus. (IV.179-183)

In bringing together physical structures on different sides of the world (Gloucester Bay and Marseilles), Eliot gives us an analogy for his juxtaposing of Krishna and Mary. This juxtaposition is not limited to the larger structure of the poem but permeates this movement.

Eliot, quoting "figlia del tuo figlio," refers to the theophany in the last canto of Paradiso, but that is not the only theophany cited in the movement. Arjuna, convinced of Krishna's godhead, says to him:

Thou art indeed just as Thou hast described Thyself, Parameshvara. I do crave to behold now that form of Thine as Ishvara. If, Lord, Thou thinkest it possible for me to bear the sight, reveal to me, O Yogeshvara, Thy imperishable form. The Lord said: Behold, O Partha, my forms divine in their hundreds and thousands, infinitely diverse, infinitely various in color and aspect. (Bhavagad Gita 11.3-4)

Arjuna requests vision of the ultimate reality. Perhaps he should not have done so, for the Lord appears to him as Vishnu, the destroyer. Arjuna recoils in horror:

For as I behold Thee touching the sky, glowing, numerous-hued, with gaping mouths and wide resplendent eyes, I feel oppressed in my innermost being. No peace nor quiet I find, O Vishnu! And as I see Thy mouths with fearful jaws, resembling the Fire of Doom, I lose all sense of direction, and find no relief. Be gracious, O Devesha, O Jagannivasa! All the sons of Dhritarashtra, and with them the crowd of kings — Bhisma, Drona, and that Karna too, as also our chief warriors — Are hastening into the fearful jaws of Thy terrible mouths. Some, indeed, caught between Thy teeth are seen, their heads being crushed to atoms. As rivers in their numerous torrents headlong to the sea, even so the heroes of the world of men rush into Thy flaming mouths.

146

The Lord said: Doom am I, full-ripe, dealing death to the worlds, engaged in devouring mankind. Even without thy slaying them, not one of the warriors ranged for battle against thee shall survive. Therefore, do thou arise, and win renown. Defeat thy foes and enjoy a thriving kingdom. By Me have these already been destroyed; be thou no more than an instrument, O Savyasachin. (Bhagavad Gita 11.24-28, 32-33)

The passage intersects with our poem at IV.180-181. Eliot prays to the Lady for those who have suffered shipwreck, but her prayer also recalls the warriors Arjuna had refused to fight who are now stuck in Vishu's teeth, a river of death bearing them to his lips. Vishnu assures Arjuna that his original impulse towards clemency was an arrogant stupidity – the god is not mocked: whether he helps or not these warriors will die and it behooves him to go with the flow rather than to kick against the pricks.

*   *   *

The story is told (in a documentary entitled "The Day After Trinity") that J. Robert Oppenheimer, as the mushroom cloud of the first atom bomb test erupted from the New Mexico desert, quoted the Bhagavad Gita 11.32 (I am become death, the destroyer of worlds). In so saying, he quoted, not Arjuna, recoiling in fear at Krishna's theophany, but the god himself. Oppenheimer recognized the mushroom cloud as humanity's theophany, that becomimg able to destroy the world humanity had joined the gods.

*   *   *

Now it is I who must offer a disclaimer. Kearns claims that the juxtaposition of Krishna and Mary in this movement constitutes a Bradlean "half-object." As she put it:

Eliot had suggested (in his doctoral thesis) that two (or more) points of view "take cognizance" of each other by each making what he called a "half-object" of the other. They see one another, as it were, from two angles at once. If such an encounter be authentic, he argued, neither point of view could emerge from it unchanged, for "strictly

147

speaking, a point of view taking note of another is no longer the same, but a third, centre of feeling."[102]

While unversed in Bradley, I know Kierkegaard's notion of a "third term" which seems analogous:

A human being is spirit. But what is spirit? Spirit is the self. But what is the self? The self is a relation that relates itself to itself, or is the relation's relating itself to itself in the relation; the self is not the relation but is the relation's relating itself to itself. A human being is a synthesis of the infinite and the finite, of the temporal and the eternal, of freedom and necessity, in short a synthesis. A synthesis is a relation between two. Considered in this way, a human being is not yet a self.

In the relation between two, the relation is the third as a negative unity, and the two relate to the relation, and in the relation to that relation; thus under the qualification of the psychical the relation between the psychical and the physical is a relation. If, however, the relation relates itself to itself, this relation is the positive third, and this is the self.[103]

Imagine a cat who, seeing herself reflected in a mirror, mistakes the image for another cat. She is body and soul in negative unity. She has a body and an animating principle, but not a self. But, if I look into the mirror, I see an image of my *self*. This self is not the body, nor is it the soul: the cat has both without having a self. The self is a relation of body and soul that is defined by neither, but by the relation between the two that allows me to relate, from a third perspective, two diverse realities into a unity. This is the positive third term.

In juxtaposing the Merciful Lady and the destroyer God, Eliot demands we see each as the completion of the other. But his "third term" is not immediately present, just as the "self" is not reflected in the mirror (or the cat would see it).[104]

*   *   *

The fourth movement, like the first, ends with a tolling bell. The first bell clangs in time to the ocean's ground swell (I.46-48). This one rings as a call to prayer in memory of the Angel's announcement to Mary. Between these two bells, is the "clamour of the bell of the last annunciation" (II.66), this bell ties the three into one as the first bell is the bell of death, the final bell the call to prayer and the middle bell represents those for whom prayers are offered.

Movement No. 5

To communicate with Mars, converse with spirits,
To report the behaviour of the sea monster,
Describe the horoscope, haruspicate or scry,
Observe disease in signatures, evoke
Biography from the wrinkles of the palm
And tragedy from fingers; release omens
By sortilege, or tea leaves, riddle the inevitable
With playing cards, fiddle with pentagrams
Or barbituric acids, or dissect
The recurrent image into pre-conscious terrors —
To explore the womb, or tomb, or dreams; all these are usual
Pastimes and drugs, and features of the press:
And always will be, some of them especially
When there is distress of nations and perplexity
Whether on the shores of Asia, or in the Edgware Road.
Men's curiosity searches past and future
And clings to that dimension. (V.184-200)

Eliot begins with a satire of the melancholy of the modern universe, empty of angels. The ancients, looking to the skies, had to imagine what *moved* them for, in their experience, things moved only as they were impelled. This is the source of the notion of supernatural movers who drive stars and planets like chariots through the sky. The advent of the impersonal forces, of gravity and inertia, left us with universe of empty mathematical space. Heavenly objects continue in motion because they were, already, in motion, nor is there any need for a first mover, because the first motion is indistinguishable from any subsequent motion.

As this is an unsatisfactory image of the cosmos (we are tales that we tell ourselves and the mathematical universe makes no sense, being an effect without a cause), there must be more to

149

the cosmos than calculus. So as scientific "explanations" fail them, leaving their questions unanswered, modern people revert to ancient superstition. Our angels become extra-terrestrials, so that we are not alone in the vast empty spaces. We seek clues to other creations in the Loch Ness monster. We attend séances, hoping to discover an afterlife. We read star charts, entrails and crystal balls. We practice divination via palmistry, I Ching, tea leaves, graphoanalysis, Tarot, Nature magick, drug-induced trances and dreams. When the meaning of the world is no longer at the center, it moves to the periphery, becoming occult.

In times of anxiety, human beings need an explanation, hope for the future no science can provide. Anxiety always revolves around *nothingness*, around the future which does not yet exist, around the emptiness of the sky. But all such researches are distraction because they do not help us to be present in the *now*, the moment of choosing.

* * *

If this movement seems to diverge from the other Quartets whose final movements are meditations on the relation of "words" to their "meanings" (allegorizing the relations of the "Word" to its "Meaning"), it is only a trick of the lights. The leading idea of this movement is *incarnation* the canonical Christian definition of which is "word made flesh."

Here, we see why Eliot brought Arjuna and Krishna into the poem. The Christian vision of incarnation is historical, describing a one time only event. This may mislead us to err in reducing the incarnation to a historical phenomenon, the misunderstanding of the search for the historical Jesus. The Gospels have the subsidiary purpose of preserving the acts and sayings of Jesus and scholars mistakenly confuse these "words" with their "meanings" as if Jesus' import were as an historical figure. Krishna and Arjuna convey us past this misconception.

As Gandhi points out, the setting of Bhagavad Gita (Arjuna and his charioteer (the disguised Lord Krishna) in the midst of what will soon be a battle field) is so obviously unhistorical we immediately see through it as a pretext.

Moreover, even if the pretext pointed to an historical event, Krishna, able to incarnate himself at will, is bound by none of his incarnations as Christ is to Jesus. Krishna continues formless, because his human form is an illusion.

Unlike the Gospels, nailed to the Cross of historical criticism, the author of the Gita freely constructs a situation illustrative of his thesis as Dante does in the Comedy. While Dante's tale takes place in a historical context (as a Christian construction) he meets Christ only at very end of his journey and then only as an incarnate mystery he cannot put into words.

Both poems make the same point: incarnation is neither theory nor historical construct, but a relationship between god and devotee. Arjuna gives himself over to the vision of Vishnu. Mary becomes the "daughter of her Son." The commonality is the insistence on surrender, of giving oneself over to a higher wisdom.

*   *   *

But to apprehend
The point of intersection of the timeless
With time, is an occupation for the saint —
No occupation either, but something given
And taken, in a lifetime's death in love,
Ardour and selflessness and self-surrender.
For most of us, there is only the unattended
Moment, the moment in and out of time,
The distraction fit, lost in a shaft of sunlight,
The wild thyme unseen, or the winter lightning
Or the waterfall, or music heard so deeply
That it is not heard at all, but you are the music
While the music lasts. (V.200-212)

The first saint Dante meets in Heaven is Piccarda Donati, a childhood friend. Her presence in Heaven is no surprise. Dante had seen her brother, Forese, in Purgatory and he had mentioned she was already there (Purgatorio 24.13-15). The surprise is, rather, that she is in the lowest heaven, the heaven of the Moon. Dante asks her:

"But tell me: though you are happy here
        Would you not desire a nearer place
        To see more and be more closely friended?"
She and the other shades smiled at me
        And she answered me with the joy
        Of one fallen in love for the first time,
"Brother, love's virtue so quiets our wills
        We desire only what we have
        Nor do we thirst for more.
Were we to aspire to a greater blessedness
        Our will would not accord
        With that of Him who placed us here.
That, as you will see, is not fitting in these circles
        The rule of love is necessary here,
        If you consider well the nature of love.
The essence of this blessed life consists
        In abiding within the limits of God's will
        Whereby our wills become one with His.
Therefore, our order of rank, from height to height,
        Throughout the realm, pleases the realm,
        And the King who makes His will our own. (Paradiso 3.64-84)
The rule of love makes heaven a paradise.

*   *   *

The ranking of saints in Dante's heaven is a matter of *condescension.* They all actually sit, at the "right hand" (so to speak) of God," but, for the purposes of our moral education, they appear in Dante's narrative sorted by their virtues. Piccarda, for instance, is in the lowest heaven as a devotee who, having offered herself in sacrifice, took herself back. After taking her vows as a Franciscan sister, her brother came to the convent and abducted her and married her off to one of his cronies. She never returned to fulfill her vow.

Beatrice has every sympathy for her capture (a person, coerced, does what they otherwise would not to *avoid* an evil and not to gain an end), but she erred in failing, once danger had passed, to return and fulfill her vow. Like Bhagavad Gita, Paradiso is all about the devotee's sacrifice of self to God.

*   *   *

Eliot makes the important, if humbling, admission that sainthood is not for everyone. This has, as its corollary, "I, myself, will never be a saint in this life." Nietzsche, arguing that God does not exist, claimed:
"If there were gods, how could I endure not to be a god! Hence, there are no gods. " [105]
With the impeccable logic of modernity any insistence that *I* am not the highest is a judgment on my personal sovereignty. This is the opposite of the rule of love, which makes another's happiness the condition of our own.

Some, by dint of an innate receptivity, hard work and God's gracious favor, attain in this life the true and abiding light of divine presence, but the rest of us must be content with, "the distraction fit, lost on a shaft of sunlight" as Eliot now refers to his vision in the garden at Burnt Norton. Such an experience is both real and unreal, real in its ecstasy, unreal in that it is falsified by any attempt to relive it. For this reason such experiences are the province of the saint alone, for only the saint has the self-discipline to accept the gift without attempting to own it.

*   *   *

These are only hints and guesses,
Hints followed by guesses; and the rest
Is prayer, observance, discipline, thought and action.
The hint half guessed, the gift half understood, is Incarnation.(V.212-215)

Again with the disclaimers! Before he will tell us the substance of devotion (prayer, observance, discipline, thought and action) he makes sure we understand he is not speaking from authority. This is a poem, not a sermon. He has not invoked God's presence (in the hope we, the readers, will do so on our own). You are the music, while the music lasts, the hint half-guessed, half-understood as incarnation.

*   *   *

Here the impossible union
Of spheres of existence is actual,
Here the past and future
Are conquered, and reconciled,
Where action were otherwise movement
Of that which is only moved
And has in it no source of movement –
Driven by daemonic, chthonic
Powers. And right action is freedom
From past and future also.
For most of us, this is the aim
Never here to be realised;
Who are only undefeated
Because we have gone on trying;
We, content at the last
If our temporal reversion nourish
(Not too far from the yew-tree)
The life of significant soil. (V.212-233)

Here – where is here? When we say "here" do we mean a place in time or space? The impossible union can be located in neither time nor space. It is, rather, the "place" where I am both object perceived and organ of perception, the self. Here -- the home of good or evil -- the soul finds its animating principle in the Spirit of God, or in the elemental spirits of the air (Ephesians 2.2).

*   *   *

To be humble (from humus) is to be grounded in the earth, and that is far from having our end in ourselves. It is the recognition that we possess, in ourselves, no power to reach our goal. As one cannot live on bread alone, our source of motion is not a something that is merely moved, but also the word, which

154

is both still *and* moving. We are still in that we have not chosen our goal: faith is in the waiting, as is humility. We are moving in that we strive constantly, knowing striving brings us no nearer the goal but makes the goal a reality, bringing it into the here and now.

St. John's at Little Gidding

Little Gidding

Here power failed my high fantasy
  Already my desire and will revolving
  Like a perfectly balanced wheel
By the love that moves the sun and other stars. (Para. 33.142-145)
Dante's journey ended with his return to earth, his will and
desire realigned and revolving in balance. Nietzsche also had
Zarathustra speak of a like journey through three realms where
his will was reformed and ending:

  The child is innocence and forgetting, a new beginning, a
game, a self-propelled wheel, a first movement, a sacred "Yes." For the
game of creation, my brothers, a sacred "Yes" is needed: the spirit now
wills his own will, and he who has been lost to the world now conquers
his own world.[106]

Nietzsche followed, in his fragmented way, Dante's
footsteps and was destroyed. We sympathize the more with his
fate as we recognize wisdom as a function of the collective, not
the individual. Dante, supported by a culture that allowed him
to enter into the highest vision and return unscathed, relied, for
his strength, on a great cloud of witnesses. Nietzsche, stumbling
alone beneath a burden too great for a man to bear, was crushed.

This supports Eliot's thesis: wisdom cannot be pursued
in isolation, but requires a community of support. In times of
cultural contest, even modern people can make common cause
against an enemy, but lacking a foe *and* a common logos the
modern world is at odds with itself. The enemy is us.

*   *   *

Little Gidding is an obscure place for a good reason. Not
that nothing important happened there, but nothing that *changed*
our world happened there. Our histories too often degenerate
into lists of the antecedents to our own situation with events
without echo in our own age left unacknowledged. The Little
Gidding community took a principled stand on the "wrong"
side of history and was destroyed, a moment pregnant with
promise that gave birth to the wind.

*   *   *

When the Nineteenth Century Oxford Movement revived High Anglicanism, religious communities were founded on a monastic model. Little Gidding had been, in the Seventeenth Century, an indigenous attempt to reinvent the religious order in England. Nicholas Ferrar founded at Little Gidding a High Anglican religious community based, not on the monastery, but the village. The community, of men and women, husbands, wives and celibates, children and elders, worked the fields and gathered three times a day to pray. Their churchmanship put them at risk in the schismatic politics of the English Civil War.

*   *   *

England's religio-political schizophrenia had not ended with the Tudors. The Stuarts, following them, shared little else other than the belief in absolute monarchy. When James, son of Mary of Scots, succeeded Elizabeth, he fled the Presbyterian Kirk as if escaping a prison, embracing the High Anglican episcopate as his vehicle of rule. The Kirk, ruled by clerical synods, was proudly independent of the crown. The Anglican episcopate made James, as "Defender of the Faith," head of State *and* Church.

As founder of the dynasty, James charted its strategic course. His ambitions were threefold:
   a)   To merge his two kingdoms (England and Scotland) under the name of the Roman province (Britain).
   b)   To set up an absolutist monarchy based on the divine right of Kings.
   c)   To use religion to bind his two realms into one through a restored episcopate.
His successors achieved only a) with b) and c) bringing ruin on his House.

*   *   *

158

Ambition is a good only when allied to self-knowledge: otherwise it only leads to overreaching. The Tudors needed only to bear children to keep the throne they had seized on Bosworth Field, and, though this proved too much for them, they still managed natural deaths. By contrast, the Stuart family matriarch, Mary of Scots, fled Scotland, implicated in her husband's murder. Arriving in England, Elizabeth imprisoned her (Mary was Henry VIII's great niece and, as the Pope had put out a fatwa on Elizabeth, Mary, as a catholic with a claim to the throne, posed the childless Elizabeth a lethal threat) and finally had her beheaded for treason (implicated in an inept assassination plot against Elizabeth). Her grandson, Charles I, was convicted of treason and beheaded by the English Parliament. Her great-grandson, James II, was deposed by a usurper who, tied to him by blood *and* marriage, looked the other way as he fled to France. The Stuarts were never as clever as they supposed themselves to be.

*   *   *

The most tragic of the Stuarts, Charles I, appears in our poem three times, as a "broken king" (LG I.26) and as a king at nightfall, and among the three on the scaffold (LG III.175-176). After his defeat at Naseby (1645), Charles fled to Little Gidding seeking and receiving sanctuary. He thus, unwittingly, delivered the Judas kiss. As High Anglicans, the Parliamentarians already suspected the Little Gidding community as a fifth column. Their hospitality to the traitor king was the last straw. A year later Parliamentary troops dispersed the community and razed the Chapel. The present Chapel is a subsequent rebuild.

*   *   *

Though critics have claimed Eliot tired while writing The Dry Salvages and regained his form in Little Gidding,[107] Eliot saw the matter differently:
My suspicions about the poem are partly due to the fact that it is written to complete a series, and not solely for itself, it may be too

much from the head and may show signs of flagging . . . . The question is not so much whether it is as good as the others (I am pretty sure it is not) but whether it is good enough to keep company with them to complete the shape. If the problem is more than one of improving details, it will have to go into storage for some time to come.[108]

Eliot's editor had received the first typescript of The Dry Salvages on January 1, 1941, before he was aware that Eliot had begun writing. The proof for publication was dated January 29, 1941 and the completed poem published before the end of February. Eliot moved on immediately to Little Gidding, wrote a single typescript and shelved the project for a year.

*　　　*　　　*

The reasons for the tabling were legion. Eliot suffered recurrent colds and chronic bronchitis, tooth extractions and fittings for dental plates. He had Vestry duties, work on a Christian newsletter, literary anthologies to edit, lectures to deliver, his duties as an air raid warden and a trip to Sweden. Further, the *strain* made certain Little Gidding would be his last poem: he could write plays in off hours while doing other things, but poetry required blocks of time and intense concentration. Time is a scarce commodity, especially when rationed, and, as Eliot often lamented, with age, concentration *goes.*

*　　　*　　　*

But I suspect the *ambition* of the project as the overriding stressor. If we use the Divine Comedy as an analogy (with Burnt Norton corresponding to Vita Nuova), we see what Eliot was up against. Inferno-Purgatorio share a common correlative: the Earth. Inferno remorselessly explores justice (and fraud) as Dante descends into a pit. Purgatorio explores grace (and art) as Dante climbs a mountain. Paradiso breaks with the established correlative as Dante, forsaking the earth, ascends into the heavens. Heaven is a synthesizing image through which Dante seeks to describe a grace that is justice and a justice that is grace. It is meant to tie off Inferno-Purgatorio into a single, neat and comprehensive bundle (Inferno-Purgatorio having already solved the problem of the Vita Nuovo). Eliot attempts a like creative summary and synthesis in Little Gidding.

Eliot announced this aim in movement IV of The Dry Salvages. The combined image of Our Lady (grace) *and* Lord Vishnu (justice) alerted us to expect an attempt at a grand synthesis. That Eliot got cold feet at the prospect of having to deliver on this promise is to be expected. Dante wrote his misgivings into the text of Paradiso, making it a tissue of excuses for his inability to do what he actually accomplished. Eliot spares us that, but did not spare himself a dozen typescripts and endless tiny adjustments to his text.

*   *   *

Once again, we consider a community, that of poetic tradition. It may seem strange that the apostle of impersonality got the "yips" contemplating himself raked over the coals by critics considering whether his influence on the tradition had been altogether salutary. This, after all, had been *his* stock and trade (we can imagine a wise guy poet of the future parodying "not with a bang but a whimper" as Eliot did "O dark dark dark."). But imitation is also flattery.

As he parodied Passage to India in The Dry Salvages, so here he parodies Dante's Inferno and Purgatorio. As he poked fun there at those who try to "converse with spirits" (DS V.184), here he has his own converse with the dead. As we say of the dead that they are "history," so Eliot peers into the abyss to the loss of individuation death affords. Soon he will no longer be an individual, subsumed into the "compound ghost" of poetic tradition. The dead will speak, their communication "tongued with fire," and, like Dante's shades, prophesy a future that has, already, come to pass: Eliot will taste the bitter ashes already on his lips, the death of creeping decrepitude.

*   *   *

The trilling wire in the blood

Sings below inveterate scars
Appeasing long forgotten wars. (BN II.49-51)

As the bombs Eliot watched fall on a ruined London do not fall on us, we likely miss the urgency of his imagery. Like Dante, for whom exile was no allegory, so, for Eliot, fire is no mere metaphor. His London hellscape has less poetry to it than we are like to think. Likewise, the parallel between Little Gidding, ruined by Civil War, and London of the Blitz is less poetic than we suppose. One must ask, however, how "forgotten" those wars can be when our blood bears the "trilling wire" of anger, pride and envy that are their source?

*   *   *

Fire purges and purifies, cleansing impurities from raw ore and making it useable. To this end Eliot quotes Julian of Norwich's famous line, "Sin is behovely," (that is, useful or necessary) for without sin there would be nothing for the fire to consume. This doctrine of *felix culpa* (the happy fault) is one of the many paradoxes that prompt thought by bringing it to a stop. It provokes thought so long as it is not of mind alone nor sings a lasting song.

The flame is a source of suffering, and Eliot pointedly reminds us that, while the fire is one, the flame has two effects: consuming the dross and cleansing the metal.

*   *   *

As the poems progressed, Eliot has questioned the commitments that hold society together: in Burnt Norton, erotic love; in East Coker and The Dry Salvages, the family; and here, in Little Gidding, nationality. The last is particularly fraught for Eliot, an Englishman by choice and not by birth. He surrendered citizenship to subject himself to a monarchy his ancestors had repudiated. Moreover, the king to whom he had pledged allegiance was facing extinction. This possibility was not unforeseen: when Eliot first chose to stay on that foggy isle, England was at war on the Continent and many crowned heads

162

fell in the aftermath. With the Battle of Britain undecided, is it surprising Eliot chose Little Gidding, a community destroyed in a civil war to focus his thoughts? What if we lose the war? What then?

Movement No. 1

Distance differentiates the opening movement of Little Gidding from the other Quartets. Burnt Norton's opening trames events in the rear-view mirror of memory (dust on a bowl of rose leaves (BN I.15)). East Coker's vision of dancing ghosts is seen only if we do not come too close (EC I.24). The Dry Salvages distances us by prosaic language and ironic disclaimers (DS 1.1-10). In Little Gidding we are dropped directly into a moment of vision in a transfigured churchyard where nature and spirit are synthesized into a single image of a newly realized immediacy. It seems contradictory (like the juxtaposition of the Virgin and Vishnu, (DS IV)), but perfectly states the poet aims.

* * *

Midwinter spring is its own season
Sempiternal though sodden towards sundown,
Suspended in time, between pole and tropic.
When the short day is brightest, with frost and fire,
The brief sun flames the ice, on pond and ditches,
In windless cold that is the heart's heat,
Reflecting in a watery mirror
A glare that is blindness in the early afternoon.
And glow more intense than blaze of branch, or brazier,
Stirs the dumb spirit: no wind, but pentecostal fire
In the dark time of the year. Between melting and freezing
The soul's sap quivers. There is no earth smell
Or smell of living thing. This is the spring time
But not in time's covenant. Now the hedgerow
Is blanched for an hour with transitory blossom
Of snow, a bloom more sudden

163

Than that of summer, neither budding nor fading,
Not in the scheme of generation.
Where is the summer, the unimaginable
Zero summer? (I.1-20)

The seeming contradiction of midwinter spring reminds us of the first lines of the second movement of East Coker:
What is the late November doing
With the disturbance of the spring (EC II.51-52)
There, Eliot asked why the confusion of youth (spring) had persisted into his dotage (late November). Here, a supernatural *brightness* invades a gathering natural gloom. In spring we celebrate the light's triumph over darkness as days lengthen. Here, day is bright though brief. We recall a poem by Yeats:
My fiftieth year had come and gone,
I sat, a solitary man,
In a crowded London shop,
An open book and empty cup
On the marble table-top.
While on the shop and street I gazed
My body of a sudden blazed;
And twenty minutes more or less
It seemed, so great my happiness, (Yeats, Vacillation)
Though the landscape differs (a London bookshop as opposed to a country churchyard), the theme remains unmistakable: the eruption of a timeless happiness into time.

*   *   *

In Eliot's midwinter spring, supernature (sempiternal) and nature (sodden toward sundown) collide. Supernature does not abolish nature, but suffuses it. A thermometer cannot measure its warmth, as it is the heart's heat. Its luminosity is not to be compared to blaze of branch or brazier. In midwinter, as in spring, sap quivers. In spring, it quivers in nature's cycle of generation:
Keeping time,
Keeping the rhythm in their dancing
As in their living in the living seasons

The time of the seasons and the constellations
The time of milking and the time of harvest
The time of the coupling of man and woman
And that of beasts. Feet rising and falling.
Eating and drinking. Dung and death.
Dawn points, and another day
Prepares for heat and silence. (EC I.39-48)

"Another day," in East Coker, fulfills the temporal contract. Here, midwinter spring is not in time's "covenant," transcending the cycles of generation and decay. The sap rises not in a tree that is merely living, but within the soul which is sempiternal.

*   *   *

Pentecostal fire recalls, not only the founding of the Church, but also the tower of Babel. The two stories operate on opposed axes: the one describing an ascent followed by a scattering, the other a descent followed by a gathering. The story of the Tower begins with the human race as a single community with one language and culture:

And as men migrated from the east, they found a plain in the land of Shinar and settled there. And they said to one another, "Come, let us make bricks, and burn them thoroughly." And they had brick for stone, and bitumen for mortar. Then they said, "Come, let us build ourselves a city, and a tower with its top in the heavens, and let us make a name for ourselves, lest we be scattered abroad upon the face of the whole earth." And the LORD came down to see the city and the tower, which the sons of men had built. And the LORD said, "Behold, they are one people, and they have all one language; and this is only the beginning of what they will do; and nothing that they propose to do will now be impossible for them. Come, let us go down, and there confuse their language, that they may not understand one another's speech." So the LORD scattered them abroad from there over the face of all the earth, and they left off building the city. Therefore its name was called Babel, because there the LORD confused the language of all the earth; and from there the LORD scattered them abroad over the face of all the earth. (Genesis 11.2-9)

Human hubris reaches into the heavens vaulting upward on the back of architecture and halted only by a disordering of *logos*. God disarms humanity by dividing it into warring factions split by divergent languages and customs.

When the day of Pentecost had come, they were all together in one place. And suddenly a sound came from heaven like the rush of a mighty wind, and it filled all the house where they were sitting. And there appeared to them tongues as of fire, distributed and resting on each one of them. And they were all filled with the Holy Spirit and began to speak in other tongues, as the Spirit gave them utterance. Now there were dwelling in Jerusalem Jews, devout men from every nation under heaven. And at this sound the multitude came together, and they were bewildered, because each one heard them speaking in his own language. And they were amazed and wondered, saying, "Are not all these who are speaking Galileans? And how is it that we hear, each of us in his own native language? Parthians and Medes and Elamites and residents of Mesopotamia, Judea and Cappadocia, Pontus and Asia, Phrygia and Pamphylia, Egypt and the parts of Libya belonging to Cyrene, and visitors from Rome, both Jews and proselytes, Cretans and Arabians, we hear them telling in our own tongues the mighty works of God." (The Acts of the Apostles 2.1-11)

The dove descends healing the wound of the Tower of Babel, calling a new people out of the warring nations by the gift of tongues of Pentecostal fire.

*   *   *

If midwinter spring is its own season, we cannot say the same of the spring. Spring is the transition from winter cold to summer heat. So nature cycles with the turning earth and the cycle encompasses human life. Midwinter spring makes the soul yearn for the "unimaginable zero summer," the resolution of the enigma of eternal arising within temporal winter. The yearning ardor for its object, through motion, attains it in stillness. The "zero summer," the longed-for object, is both present and not yet, experienced, though not grasped.

*   *   *

If you came this way,
Taking the route you would be likely to take
From the place you would be likely to come from,
If you came this way in may time, you would find the hedges
White again, in May, with voluptuary sweetness.
It would be the same at the end of the journey,
If you came at night like a broken king,
If you came by day not knowing what you came for,
It would be the same, when you leave the rough road
And turn behind the pig-sty to the dull facade
And the tombstone. And what you thought you came for
Is only a shell, a husk of meaning
From which the purpose breaks only when it is fulfilled
If at all. Either you had no purpose
Or the purpose is beyond the end you figured
And is altered in fulfilment. There are other places
Which also are the world's end, some at the sea jaws,
Or over a dark lake, in a desert or a city –
But this is the nearest, in place and time
Now and in England. (I.20-39)

Now we transcend temporal sequence as the first voice speaks from the churchyard, the second is still on the way. Eliot visited Little Gidding only once, in May 1936. He arrived when the hedges were white, not with snow as "before," but with "voluptuary sweetness" (the "prior" visit occurred "not in time's covenant").

He arrives at the end of his journey to discover that the *end* is not its *purpose*. He has come there, not simply to be there, but now he must ask what he is there *for*.

*   *   *

What must it have been to have arrived there as a broken king, fleeing the battle that had dashed his fortunes? No longer driven by the pomp of princely power, he flees as one stung, reeling in grief for a lost army: who died on his command. He flees the wrath of treacherous subjects whose hatred marshaled

167

thousands to his defeat. Say what you will of Richard III: he had the good sense to die on Bosworth Field, a good sense Charles, at Naseby, richly lacked.

As Arjuna despaired of killing so many loved ones on the field of Kuru, so Charles' heart sank at Naseby. They differ in that the field of Kuru was, for Arjuna, also the field of Dharma: he despaired *before* the battle, allowing Krishna to restore his resolve. Charles, having destroyed his army, compounded his mistake by fleeing to Little Gidding.

*   *   *

In a sense, *where* we come from does not matter, but the destination. In a sense, *where* we are going does not matter, but that we are on the way. The destination always changes in time, if we are attentive to the time. It changes as we change so it changes en route. We are not who we were when we set out, so our destination changes, not by becoming a different place, but a place we will *perceive* differently. We may arrive by night, like a broken king fleeing a debacle. We may arrive by day as an aging, disappointed poet who had imagined the place in a romantic haze, disabused by the pig sty, tombstone and dull facade. However we arrive, we arrive as a pilgrim who, having surrendered her safe, home identity, now finds herself no one on the way to nowhere.

*   *   *

Art prompted Eliot's pilgrimage. A year after his success with Murder in the Cathedral a friend, George Every, brought him his own English-historical-religious verse play, *Stalemate: the King at Little Gidding*. Throughout the year, Eliot commented on the drafts and, in May, went to the site to pick up its flavor. It is also from this manuscript that Eliot began to associate Little Gidding with fire.

In the play, one of the characters imaged the Civil war as a forest fire, and the lead character, John Ferrar, (nephew of the deceased founder, Nicholas) took up the image, wondering whether to walk away from or *through* the fire. A Parliamentary officer warned him to stand clear: God, by giving the Parliamentarians victory, has shown whom He favors. John grants the Parliamentarian victory was God's will, but is less certain of God's purposes. As he and his friends pray for guidance, the king interrupts them, seeking sanctuary. They extend hospitality at their community's expense.

*   *   *

What can the journey mean? We did not come for the scenery. We returned from the beautiful garden at Burnt Norton with a pocketful of rose leaves and regrets. Here no beauty arrests our eyes: only an ordinary, not very graceful country church. What did we come here looking for? What did the king come looking for? The end of the journey is not its meaning, nor is the meaning a souvenir we can take home with us.

We must learn from our mistake in the rose garden, when we had the experience and mistook its meaning for an earthly object. The end of the journey is not its meaning – or, rather, the end is inseparable from the journey itself. Nor was it anything we would have anticipated before the journey.

Arriving, we have reached the end of the world. There are many such places:

The 'sea's jaws' he associated with Iona and St. Columba and with Lindisfarne and St. Cuthbert: the 'dark lake' with the lake of Glendalough and St. Kevin's hermitage in County Wicklow: the desert with the hermits of the Thebaid and St. Antony: the city with Padua and the other St. Antony." [109]

But this is the nearest: now and in England. Yeats had claimed that our insistence on historical holy lands had robbed all lands and denied their inhabitants the right to find God in their own, indigenous landscapes. [110] Like Chaucer, Eliot finds the end of his pilgrimage in England, but, in the Modern Age, pilgrimage is no longer a recognized social institution. He must find his own way to the end of the world.

The end of the world is a place to die and to be reborn. The "end of the world" is no place of great echoing noise: it is far

169

from the field of battle, a place to flee the battle. The world turns not on the great noises of history. It turns *inaudibly*.

*   *   *

If you came this way,
Taking any route, starting from anywhere,
At any time or at any season,
It would always be the same: you would have to put off
Sense and notion. You are not here to verify,
Instruct yourself, or inform curiosity
Or carry report. You are here to kneel
Where prayer has been valid. And prayer is more
Than an order of words, the conscious occupation
Of the praying mind, or the sound of the voice praying.
And what the dead had no speech for, when living,
They can tell you, being dead: the communication
Of the dead is tongued with fire beyond the language of the living.
Here, the intersection of the timeless moment
Is England and nowhere. Never and always. (I.39-53)

Home is where we start from (EC V.190). In Eliot's case, St. Louis, Missouri; in yours, you supply the place. It does not matter where we start from as the journey is the same. Our purpose is not to narrate or explain: our journey cannot be described in words. We are not here to get anything we can take home with us. We have come to a place where prayer has been valid, though the place itself has been overthrown. Though winning and losing reflect the will of God, that will remains inscrutable: we can only try to bring ourselves into harmony with it. Hence, *prayer*. We are here to *pray*, and prayer is no form of words, no intentional act of body or soul, but the attunement of all our faculties as we open ourselves to the presence of God. Prayer, then, is no act of will to be enacted, except in the sense that it is the will not to act. Prayer is *validated*, not by our gaining that for which we asked, but in emptying ourselves in surrender to God.

We open ourselves to God, not in one-on-one conversation, but among the many. We are here to find our place among the saints, to become one among the great cloud of witnesses. With Bernard, who has never burned so for his own vision as for ours, among the saints who, folding their hands, beg that we be allowed to reach our destination.

Movement No. 2

Modernity values material achievement over spiritual striving. Descartes heralded the move from the Middle Ages to Modernity in his transition from "the speculative philosophy taught in the schools," to a "practical" science enabling us to become "lords and masters of Nature." As the desire for scarce natural goods (especially when pursued competitively in a zero-sum game) is endless, we become, not lords and masters, but addicts. The more energy we dig up, the more ways we find to consume it and the more we *need* to dig up.

Concentration on the advancement of the material at the expense of the spiritual has built an inverse Tower of Babel. At Babel, humankind, sharing one logos, was so united in the pursuit of God that God, as *prey*, had to end the hunt. Here, humankind, bearing competing logoi, battle over the resources of an increasingly limited planet (population exploding as resources are depleted).

*   *   *

War has always had dire consequences for civilian populations: when one army destroyed another, any nearby village or town was sacked, slaves taken, women raped. But now a new phrase enters the English language: terror bombing, that is, terror as a tactic aimed at destroying the civilian population's will to resist. Hitler bombed London nightly, hoping vainly:

1) To steal the sky from the RAF, enabling a land invasion (Hitler did not know the RAF had a secret weapon, radar, allowing them to stay one step ahead of his Luftwaffe).

171

2) To turn public opinion against war (People surrender hoping for mercy: the nightly bombing sent the wrong signal. Daily reminded of Hitler's ruthlessness, they *feared* to surrender.).

We have emerged into a new age of barbarism: the age of total war. War, no longer restricted to combatants and those unfortunates whose lives and property are forfeit as the "spoils" of a victorious army (the ancient and medieval version of "collateral damage"), but civilians are intentionally targeted. Is there a real distinction between "total war" and "state sponsored terrorism?" Is the difference more than that one group hijacks airplanes and the other flies sorties on a schedule?

*   *   *

In East Coker's first movement Elyot ghosts dance. In Little Gidding's second the elements dance. Both dances circle around a fire. The dance of the elements "beginning" in the word "ash" and "ending" on the word "fire," encloses the circle. They differ as the Elyots dance to a sensual love that is "dung and death," while the elements dance around the purgatorial fire of rebirth.

*   *   *

Ash on and old man's sleeve
Is all the ash the burnt roses leave.
Dust in the air suspended
Marks the place where a story ended.
Dust inbreathed was a house –
The walls, the wainscot and the mouse,
The death of hope and despair,
This is the death of air. (II.54-61)

Eliot, who wrote a poem entitled "Ash Wednesday," knew, all too well, the Priest's mantra as he or she smears ash on penitent foreheads: "Remember thou art dust and to dust thou shalt return." Human life is a proverb of impermanence, at least, as it is "woven in the weakness of the changing body" (BN II.79).

The cycle of ash, from Palm Sunday exultation to Ash Wednesday penitence, passes through Holy Saturday flames. The false triumph of Palm Sunday, of Jesus' entry as Jerusalem's earthly king, is humbled with the lighting of a new fire at the vigil of resurrection. Into the flames go exultant hopes of earthly glory to resurface, at the other end of the year, as penitential ash.

*   *   *

The ash, here, is not of palm, but of the rose. Asked the significance of the rose, Eliot answered:

There are really three roses in the set of poems, the sensuous rose, the social-political Rose (always appearing with the capital letter) and the spiritual rose: and the three have got to somehow be identified as one.[111]

Each of the first three Quartets introduce a rose. The sensual rose emerged in Burnt Norton, the spiritual rose in East Coker and the social-political Rose in The Dry Salvages. All the roses reappear in Little Gidding: the sensual rose here as ash; the socio-political Rose at III.184 as a specter; the spiritual rose as its culmination at V.259.

*   *   *

The ash is hardly sacramental and, perhaps, less than symbolic. Eliot recalled:

During the Blitz the accumulated debris was suspended in the London air for hours after the bombing. Then it would slowly descend and cover one's sleeves and coat with a fine white ash. I often experienced this effect during long night hours on the roof.[112]

The rose of Burnt Norton is reduced to ash. The house, wainscot and mouse of East Coker are reduced to dust. This death of air is the death of love in Burnt Norton *and* the death of earth in East Coker, the city *replaced* by a pile of rubble. When we recall that the writing of Little Gidding was interrupted by recurrent bouts of bronchitis, we recognize the death of air calls attention to Eliot's sacrifice in breathing his death.

There are flood and drouth
Over the eyes and in the mouth,
Dead water and dead sand
Contending for the upper hand.
The parched eviscerate soil
Gapes at the vanity of toil,
Laughs without mirth.
This is the death of earth. (II.62-69)

Shakespeare's second tetralogy of history plays (Richard II, Henry IV 1 and 2, Henry V) are prequel to his first (Henry VI 1, 2 and 3, Richard III). An epilogue ends Henry V, connecting them:

Small time, but in that small most greatly lived
This star of England: Fortune made his sword;
By which the world's best garden be achieved,
And of it left his son imperial lord.
Henry the Sixth, in infant bands crown'd King
Of France and England, did this king succeed;
Whose state so many had the managing,
That they lost France and made his England bleed. (Henry V 5. 2).

Henry V ends in triumph because it does not follow Henry beyond his thirtieth birthday. He would die on campaign seven years later and all he gained was lost.

*   *   *

Every great man experiences the death of air in his reflection. As Solomon said:

Then I saw that wisdom excels folly as light excels darkness. The wise man has his eyes in his head, but the fool walks in darkness; and yet I perceived that one fate comes to all of them. Then I said to myself, "What befalls the fool will befall me also; why then have I been so very wise?" .... I hated all my toil in which I had toiled under the sun, seeing that I must leave it to the man who will come after me; and who knows whether he will be a wise man or a fool? Yet he will be

master of all for which I toiled and used my wisdom under the sun.
This also is vanity. (Ecclesiastes 2.13-15, 17-19)
A mighty man may, by will and skill, contend with and conquer the world, but lose it all if, when he dies, he leaves it to a mouse. To die is to surrender the world absolutely, but as love persists beyond the grave in grief, so attachment anticipates loss in anxiety. Attachment to self and things and persons must feel the "sting" of loss, as all these must be surrendered in death. This is "laughter without mirth," the death of earth.

*   *   *

Water and fire succeed
The town, the pasture and the weed.
Water and fire deride
The sacrifice that we denied.
Water and fire shall rot
The marred foundations we forgot,
Of sanctuary and choir.
This is the death of water and fire. (II.70-77)
 Water and fire take us beyond the death of the body (air) and the death of the soul (earth) to a new spiritual realm. Water and fire are not only Heraclitean opposites, but water, in the oceans, symbolizes the eternal and fire, the means of sacrifice. The water and fire deride the sacrifice that we denied, offering a true sacrifice. The sacrifice of Little Gidding, offered by the Parliamentarians, is a false sacrifice: an offering in lieu of the self. The only true offering is the offering of the self to the eternal by fire. By offering God less, we build Churches with marred foundations that, in judgment, water and fire rot.

*   *   *

 When I affirm that more can be learned about how to write poetry from Dante than from any English poet, I do not at all mean that Dante's way is the only right way, or that Dante is thereby <u>greater</u> than Shakespeare or, indeed any other English poet. I put my meaning into other words by saying that Dante can do less <u>harm</u> to anyone

175

trying to learn to write verse than can Shakespeare. Most great English poets are <u>inimitable</u> in a way Dante was not. If you try to imitate Shakespeare you will certainly produce a series of stilted, forced and violent distortions of language. The language of each great English poet is his own language; the language of Dante is the perfection of a common language. In a sense, it is more pedestrian that of Dryden or Pope. If you follow Dante without talent, you will be at worse pedestrian and flat; if you follow Shakespeare or Pope without talent, you will make an utter fool of yourself.[113]

Eliot, writing in 1929, did not anticipate that he would ever be so daft as to attempt a full on Dante parody. The technical difficulties were daunting. Terza rima, the poetic form Dante invented for his Comedy, was meant for Italian. English is ill-adapted to it, being less fecund in rhyme and what rhyme there is, more *emphatic*. So Eliot attempted to replicate Dante's rhyme by alternating unrhymed masculine and feminine word endings.

The greater difficulty, however, was the *rigor* of the form. As Eliot put it, terza rima is so spare and angular a style that "the slightest vagueness or imprecision is immediately noticeable." Eliot noted, with a seeming satisfaction, this passage "not the length of one canto of the Divine Comedy – cost me far more time and trouble and vexation than any passage of the same length that I have ever written." [114]

*　　*　　*

In the uncertain hour before the morning
Near the ending of interminable night
At the recurrent end of the unending
After the dark dove with the flickering tongue
Had passed below the horizon of his homing
While the dead leaves still rattled on like tin
Over the asphalt where no other sound was
Between three districts whence the smoke arose
I met one walking, loitering and hurried
As if blown towards me like the metal leaves
Before the urban dawn wind unresisting.

And as I fixed upon the down-turned face
That pointed scrutiny with which we challenge
    The first-met stranger in the waning dusk
    I caught the sudden look of some dead master
Whom I had known, forgotten, half recalled
    Both one and many; in the brown baked features
    The eyes of a familiar compound ghost
Both intimate and unidentifiable.
    So I assumed a double part, and cried
    And heard another's voice cry: 'What! are you here?'
Although we were not. I was still the same,
    Knowing myself yet being someone other —
    And he a face still forming; yet the words sufficed
To compel the recognition they preceded.
    And so, compliant to the common wind,
    Too strange to each other for misunderstanding,
In concord at this intersection time
    Of meeting nowhere, no before and after,
    We trod the pavement in a dead patrol.
I said: 'The wonder that I feel is easy,
    Yet ease is cause of wonder. Therefore speak:
    I may not comprehend, may not remember.'
And he: 'I am not eager to rehearse
    My thoughts and theory which you have forgotten.
    These things have served their purpose: let them be.
So with your own, and pray they be forgiven
    By others, as I pray you to forgive
    Both bad and good. Last season's fruit is eaten
And the fullfed beast shall kick the empty pail.
    For last year's words belong to last year's language
    And next year's words await another voice. (II.78-119)

      The terza rima of the second movement is, like the lyric
of the fourth movement of The Dry Salvages, in two parts. And,
like that lyric, they refer to two differing understandings of one
reality. The first 42 lines of Eliot's terza rima describe a hellscape.
The final thirty are a redemptive vision (Purgatory). The two
differ as a photograph from its negative.[115]

           *   *   *

177

As with the dead sestina of the second movement of The Dry Salvages, we begin with dead terza rima, lines so metrically monotonous as to be lifeless. As Dante began his poem in the middle of the journey that is our life, so Eliot begins at the end of interminable night.

*   *   *

Dante, with the dawn, looked up to a hopeful vision:
But when I reached the foot of a hill,
   Where ended that wooded valley
   That had pierced my heart with fear,
Looking up, I saw her shoulders shawled
   Already by the first beams of the planet
   That leads us straight on every road.
Then the fear somewhat subsided,
   That had roiled the lake of my heart
   All through the anguished night. (Inferno 1.13-21)
Eliot looked up into the interminable night and saw a dread object: the dark dove. Each Quartet has its birds: Burnt Norton, its deceiving thrush and kingfisher; East Coker, its absent early owl and soaring petrel; The Dry Salvages, its yelping sea gull. Here the bird, the dark dove, is man-made. Prior birds have symbolized wisdom. This bird, the image of technology, is a weapon of mass-destruction.

*   *   *

Eliot continually refers to Inferno 15, Dante's meeting with Brunetto Latini among the sodomites (not homosexuals, an anachronistic coinage of the Nineteenth Century). The meeting with Brunetto occurs on a burning plain beneath raining fire. The fiery rain punishes those who abused nature and sodomy was seen as such an abuse. Images of turning imply a sexual relation between the two men that, once ended, also ended Dante's experimentation with sodomy: unlike Lot's wife, he did not turn back (Inferno 15.15). His dismay at seeing Brunetto among the damned indicates he had hoped Brunetto had done the same, but he is disappointed (Inferno 15.33). [116]

Eliot contemplates a like fiery rain from the "dark dove with the flickering tongue." Having dropped his lethal cargo, he wings his way "below the horizon of his homing" as his droppings break into shrapnel, landing on asphalt like tin. The three districts center on Lake Garda, where three dioceses (Trent, Brescia and Verona) overlap, and where any of three bishops may bless (Inferno 20.67-69). Here, the "blessing" is of a different kind. Another Dantean image immediately follows:

And we met a band of souls approaching
>   *Along the bank, each intently staring,*
>   *As people at twilight,*
Look at each other, beneath a new moon,
>   *And they sharpened their brows toward us*
>   *As an old tailor does towards the eye of a needle.*
So scrutinized by this family,
>   *I was recognized by one, who seized me*
>   *By the hem, shouting, "How marvelous!"*
And I, as he stretched his arm to me,
>   *Fixed my eyes of his baked visage*
>   *So that the scorching could not preclude*
My mind from knowing him,
>   *I lowered my face towards his face*
>   *And answered, "Are you here, Ser Brunetto?" (Inferno 15.16-*
30)

The damned "sharpen their brows" towards Dante as an old tailor squints towards the eye of a needle, and Eliot challenges the ghost with "pointed scrutiny." Eliot's sees in the "down-turned features" a composite figure made up of aspects of certain individuals and Dante, looking into a "baked visage," recognizes a dead master. The dead master tells Eliot that last year's fruit is eaten and the fullfed beast shall kick the empty pail, and Brunetto tells Dante that the grass shall be far from the goat's reach (Inferno 15.72).[117]

In the drafts Eliot directly quotes Inferno 15.30 ("Are you here, Ser Brunetto?")[118] When his editor objected to Eliot's excision of "Ser Brunetto," Eliot responded:

179

I think you will recognize that it was necessary to get rid of Brunetto for two reasons. The first is that the visionary figure has now become somewhat more definite and will no doubt be identified by some readers with Yeats though I do not mean anything so precise as that. However, I do not wish to take the responsibility of putting Yeats or anybody else into Hell and I do not want to impute to him the particular vice which took Brunetto there. Secondly, although the reference to that Canto is intended to be explicit, I wished the effect of the whole to be Purgatorial which is much more appropriate.[119]

Eliot expected the ghost to be identified with Yeats (whose body was buried[120], for a year, on a foreign shore before it was reinterred in Ireland) and he did not want to imply a) that Yeats was in Hell nor b) nor (as Dante seems to between himself and Brunetto) any sexual relations between himself and Yeats.

*   *   *

A tree there is that from its topmost bough
Is half all glittering flame and half all green
Abounding foliage moistened with the dew;
And half is half and yet is all the scene;
And half and half consume what they renew,
And he that Attis' image hangs between
That staring fury and the blind lush leaf
May know not what he knows, but knows not grief (Yeats, Vacillation)

Yeats' poem "Vacillation," gives us a taste of the thought and theory the ghost refuses to rehearse. The image of a tree, half fire and half green pictures the human being, suspended between time and eternity, between ideas and desires, hungering for both. Hence, the soul "vacillates."

Like Solomon in Ecclesiastes, Yeats suggests testing every work under the sun, knowing that any work is an "extravagance of breath\ that are not suited for such men as come\ proud, open-eyed and laughing to the tomb." The next stanza begins with a passage quoted earlier referring to the opening vision of Little Gidding: Yeats' vision in a London shop, like Eliot's in Burnt Norton, immediately collapses into recrimination. In the

180

timeless moment, he saw the possibility of his salvation, but
returning to time, he vacillates, noting his unworthiness.
Responsibility so weighs me down.
Things said or done long years ago,
Or things I did not do or say
But thought that I might say or do,
Weigh me down, and not a day
But something is recalled,
My conscience or my vanity appalled. (Yeats, Vacillation)

Recognizing ourselves as sinners is the necessary first
step, but is insufficient of itself. Humility demands a further
step: that, though we are undeserving, we accept the love that is
offered us in the forgiveness of sins. Pride says, Better a beggar
than to pay with another's coin," but Heaven is given only as an
unmerited gift.

Yeats ends "Vacilliation" with a valediction, "So get you
gone, Von Hugel, though with blessings on your head."
Choosing between von Hugel and his Medieval mystics and
Homer and his poets, Yeats dismisses von Hugel with a polite
"No, thank you." In the third movement Eliot expresses the
opposite affinity.

*   *   *

On first reading Eliot's essay, Tradition and the
Individual Talent, the doctrine seemed very familiar. Then I
remembered:
Thus as it is asserted by great sages
   That the Phoenix dies and is reborn
   As it approaches its five hundredth year. (Inferno 24.106-108)
Dante quotes a quotation. Dante quotes Ovid, who quotes
Pythagoras (Metamorphoses 15.391-417), and Eliot's ideas are
very near to theirs.

Poetry is about the individual talent only as the
individual is the living manifestation of the tradition. The living
poet is a prism refracting the tradition by his or her
individuality, but poetry remains itself by constantly
assimilating new to old. Each new poem casts the tradition in a

181

new light. Each new allusion retroactively modifies its referent. Poetry, like the Phoenix, dies to be reborn.

But this rebirth is no resurrection, but a replacement. Pythagoras is different now that Ovid has overlaid him: we cannot get him back as he was before. Ovid's insights are changed by having found a place in Dante's Christian epic. It is changed once more as Eliot introduces it into the modern context. Poetry, like the phoenix, is ever reborn from the ashes of the old.

*   *   *

The protagonist 0f Dante's Sixth heaven (the Heaven of Jupiter) is the Eagle, a composite character made up of just rulers from all times and places, that is roughly analogous to Eliot's ghost. Eliot no more considers poetry the province of the isolated individual than Dante considered justice an individual virtue. For Dante, justice is a universal, just as, for Eliot, poetry is the province of tradition.

Introduced to the exemplars of that Heaven, Dante meets, not individuals, but aspects making up the Eagle's eye. The rule of justice, like that of poetry, transcends simple individuality, entering into a fellowship transcending time and place (the exemplars are two pagans, two Jews and two Christians (Paradiso 20.34-72)).

The analogy breaks down when we consider that Dante is no king, and so, unlike Eliot confronting the effigy of poetic tradition, he cannot cry "and hear another's voice cry." The imperious Eagle's voice does not echo Dante's as Eliot's poetic voice doubles his own.

*   *   *

Eliot had criticized Milton for writing English as if it were a dead language. In these lines he shows he too can play that game:

All this evidence of the poet's failure to make the most of his materials point to no ordinary failure: there is something more to

182

Eliot's lines that arrests any simple judgment. The limitation and defects seem to me undeniable. Yet what most readers and critics find, that there is great power and authority in the verse, is not to be denied either. It is an extraordinary kind of inferior writing that can be regarded, as this passage generally is, as a supreme achievement of poetic genius. What we have to reckon with is a mastery which is not infusing new life into the versification and the language; and shows itself in precisely in not doing that – by controlling, repressing and refusing to enter into the full life of the words and of the world.[121]

Burnt Norton was a technically improved restatement of The Waste Land. Here we reach a breakthrough. Eliot has escaped his Hell, which he now recognizes as a kind of intellectual aloofness, a smug superiority that recognized the world as a trap and looked down on others too dense to notice. Such a position can only be maintained by repression. And here Eliot, in parodying Dante's Hell, parodies himself from The Waste Land to Burnt Norton. The war has brought Eliot to a new understanding: he is not to hold himself out, but give himself up. So the ghost, asked to repeat his teaching, refuses: he is better off repenting than repeating, for in repenting he has hope of forgiveness. In doing so, he sets Eliot a salutary example. The rest of the movement explains what Eliot had learned and what he has to regret.

*   *   *

But, as the passage now presents no hindrance
      To the spirit unappeased and peregrine
      Between two worlds become much like each other,
So I find words I never thought to speak
      In streets I never thought I should revisit
      When I left my body on a distant shore.
Since our concern was speech, and speech impelled us
      To purify the dialect of the tribe
      And urge the mind to aftersight and foresight,
Let me disclose the gifts reserved for age
      To set a crown upon your lifetime's effort.
      First, the cold friction of expiring sense

Without enchantment, offering no promise
  But bitter tastelessness of shadow fruit
  As body and soul begin to fall asunder.
Second, the conscious impotence of rage
  At human folly, and the laceration
  Of laughter at what ceases to amuse.
And last, the rending pain of re-enactment
  Of all that you have done, and been; the shame
  Of motives late revealed, and the awareness
Of things ill done and done to others' harm
  Which once you took for exercise of virtue.
  Then fools' approval stings, and honour stains.
From wrong to wrong the exasperated spirit
  Proceeds, unless restored by that refining fire
  Where you must move in measure, like a dancer.'
The day was breaking. In the disfigured street
  He left me, with a kind of valediction,
  And faded on the blowing of the horn. (II.120-149)

I am convinced that Eliot abandoned Little Gidding for a year primarily because he was disheartened by the uninspired first typescript of this passage. He dumped the original ghostly oracle and replaced it with the brilliant published version. In the first type script the ghost says:

Remember rather the essential moments
  That were the times of birth and death and change
  The agony and the solitary vigil
Remember also the fear, loathing and hate
  The wild strawberries eaten in the garden,
  The walls of Poitiers and the Anjou wine,
The fresh new season's rope, the smell of varnish
  On the clean oar, the drying sails,
  Such things as seem of least and most importance.
So, as you circumscribe this dreary round,
  Shall your life pass from you with all you hated
  And all you love, the future and the past.
United to another past, another future,
  (After many seas and after many lands)
  The dead and the unborn who shall be nearer
Than the voices and the faces that were most near.

This is the final gift of earth accorded –
One soil, one past, one future, in one place.
Nor shall the eternal be remoter
But nearer: seek or seek not, it is here.
Now the last love on earth. The rest is grace"
He turned away, and in the autumn weather
I heard a distant dull deferred report
At which I started: and the sun had risen.[122]

I hesitated to reprint this as Eliot fittingly placed it at the bottom of his wastebasket. He had completely regressed to Burnt Norton's "Ridiculous the waste sad time\Stretching before and after" (BN V.174-175), a waste time made palatable by the remembrance of timeless moments. It was as if East Coker and the Dry Salvages had not intervened. Perhaps Eliot had not fully entered into the spirit of necromancy: the dead predict the future, they <u>are</u> the past.

Ghosts are images of the past and availing only as they beckon to the future. Sins, forgiven, call us to forget the is past and *strive* to do better in the time left to us. Thus, in the published version, the ghost rightly warns us of what to expect and ignores the past.

*   *   *

The passage between two worlds much like each other (Hell and Purgatory) is open, and we pass between them unhindered. The channel frees the ghost's tongue to speak as never before. Hell and Purgatory differ not by sin, but by repentance, in the acceptance of offered grace. God does not await our asking to offer, but is helpless in the face of our refusal.

*   *   *

The damned have a home, but the penitent is a wanderer. The damned are still, even in their motion on the way to where already are. The penitent is on her way to a place she will recognize, though previously unseen. The souls of Purgatory are peregrine, metoikos and are, thus, unappeased: a home is a consolation prize.

*   *   *

Speech concerns the poet, and as a man cannot live by bread alone, so the word cannot be reduced to a tool. The poet must make it dance, inspiring his tribe to savor their common possession, draining its fullest expression. It must mean more than mere meaning, calling the mind to retrospect and prospect, to contemplate the self in its incompletion and to grieve that which cannot be undone.

Like Dante's shades, the compound ghost predicts a "future" that has already come to pass. Eliot has already tasted the ironical "gifts" of age, and noted the absence of the early owl (EC I.23).

The first "gift" is diminished sensation. Socrates tells Alcibiades, "The eyes of the mind sharpen just as the bodily eyes fail" (Plato, Symposium, 219a). The ghost describes this loss, paradoxically as a "bitter tastelessness." The loss of the senses makes a claustrophobic world as the self, losing its outlet, begins closing in on itself.

This leads to the second "gift." No longer enchanted by the senses, we "see" the human world, driven to feed the hungering senses, is quite mad. We participated in the madness like contestants on a game show, so beguiled by winning and losing that we took no notice of the humiliation we inflicted on ourselves and others. Only at the distance of expiring sensation does the dumb futility of the game crash in on us. Did money or status or sex really matter when the end is the grave?

The final "gift" is a lacerated conscience and shameful memories. Sensual desire is its own justification, once withdrawn, our earlier actions change their aspect. No longer transfixed by win and lose, what pride can we take in our "conquests," moments when we abased ourselves and others on a fool's errand? Praise is revalued in light of those who praised, so that "fools' approval stings, and honor stains."

186

                                    *   *   *

     The ghost returns us to Dante's depiction of Arnaut Daniel in Purgatorio 26. Daniel, though cordial, has little time to converse, too busy with the demands of his purgation. The sooner he finishes, the sooner heaven will be his, so, he dives into the flames as a fish to the bottom of a lake. He dives into purgatorial fire, the flames of charity, to cleanse himself of lust, the greater fire burning out the less.

     But Eliot's image is dancing, not diving. Perhaps, as Daniel is in the final stage of his purgation, he can afford its abandoned pursuit, but the process as a whole restores balance, order and *measure* to a soul disordered by sin. Purgation (that is, cleansing) restores primal innocence (thus the process ends in the return to Eden). In this, Piccarda is our guide, for the rule of love is the rule of Heaven and Purgatory exists to instill the rule of love in which order is perfected.

                                    *   *   *

     With the sounding of the all clear, the dawn breaks and the poetic ghost, like Hamlet's father, disappears.

Movement No. 3

There are three conditions which often look alike
Yet differ completely, flourish in the same hedgerow:
Attachment to self and to things and to persons, detachment
From self and from things and from persons; and, growing between them,
indifference
Which resembles the others as death resembles life,
Being between two lives — unflowering, between
The live and the dead nettle. (III.150-156)
     In his "parable of the nettles" Eliot returns to the imagery of the fourth movement of The Dry Salvages. There he melded Mary's gracious, feminine wisdom with Vishnu's wrathful

masculine energy into a single vision. Here he separates them in order to explore a third which is neither plenitude nor vacancy.

In the same hedgerow flourish three nettles. The live or stinging nettle, image of attachment to self, things and persons, does not flower, but injects, by its hollow hairs, a toxin in defense of the fruit of action. In this it resembles Vishnu. The dead nettle, the image of detachment from self, things and persons, having surrendered the fruit of action, has no need for self-defense and can, instead, flower. Between them lies the nettle of indifference. It takes the fruit of action mindlessly, neither offering nor refusing:

The dripping blood our only drink,
The bloody flesh our only food:
In spite of which we like to think
That we are sound, substantial flesh and blood —
Again, in spite of that, we call this Friday good. (EC IV.167-171)

The indifferent nettle takes the "medicine of salvation" unaware that it is the cure for a disease nor that he bears within himself a "distempered part" in need of it. The Mass seems a quaint and convivial ritual whose meaning passes over them like so much metaphysical poetry.

*   *   *

We did not previously question why, despite its argument urging violence, Gandhi translated the Bhagavad Gita so that Hindus, unversed in Sanskrit, could read it. Shouldn't he have suppressed it instead? He did not because he *understood* it. He saw clearly that violence-non-violence is a false dichotomy. *What* we do does not matter, but *how* we do it.

Arjuna, faced with having to kill men for whom he felt no hostility but only love and gratitude, withdrew into indifference, planning to shirk his duty. He would thus set the example that one should do one's duty only when it is no sacrifice. Lord Krishna denounced his impiety demanding Arjuna do his duty despite the pain. This is the principle Gandhi espoused, and it has to do with neither violence nor non violence, but *resolve.*

Purgatory is not the middle realm between Heaven and Hell: souls in Purgatory are as sinless as those in Heaven. The souls of Purgatory are *not* punished for their sins. Their sins are forgiven and trouble them only in memory. These memories remain and cannot be purged until they are beyond temptation. The exercises of Purgatory make the penitent aware of how sin, in the name of small, fleeting "pleasures," had defrauded him of true and lasting joy. Once she recognizes sin as the source of all her unhappiness, she is through with sin and may be purged even of the memories of past transgressions, as she is truly "a new creation."

The middle realm between Hell and Heaven is the "vestibule" of Hell. There dwell souls who lived lives of neither infamy nor praise (Inferno 3.36). They cohabit with the neutral angels who, in the heavenly war, sided with neither Satan nor God. Neutrality, as a policy, works only when neither side has the upper hand: if either side wins, the neutral lose. The victor has spoils enough to share among those who contributed to his victory. The loser sees their fence-sitting contributed to his defeat. Neither side has use for them and, when the battle is done, they are shut out by Satan <u>and</u> by God.

In Dante's day, with its overpowering logos, the indifferent could be dealt with in less than half a canto: the vast majority forced to choose sides. In the modern world, where the word is weak, the besetting danger is indifference: people who are not really bad and not really good. Hitler succeeded, not because the Germans were evil, but because most of them were *indifferent.* He was an ill wind who drove them like inert bits of paper. Absent true logos an evil man was able to become the measure of all things.

*   *   *

This is the use of memory:
For liberation — not less of love but expanding

Of love beyond desire, and so liberation
From the future as well as the past. Thus, love of a country
Begins as attachment to our own field of action
And comes to find that action of little importance
Though never indifferent. History may be servitude,
History may be freedom. See, now they vanish,
The faces and places, with the self which, as it could, loved them,
To become renewed, transfigured, in another pattern. (III.156-165)

Speaking of the use of memory we mean that called, from ancient days, sublimation, the alchemy of making the base metal of animal emotion fit to envision angels. A critic has written:

> *The drafts of The Waste Land directed attention upon a crisis of personality. They exposed the diseased state of sensibility which Eliot had to express, and they made it clear that the essential action of the poem was the process by which the sensibility gradually made itself whole. Its predicament was that of being conscious, and only being conscious of '"the horror, the horror"' of life; and its cure was to become wholly possessed by the horrors. The personality of the poet, in that poem, needed to realize itself through the intensification of suffering and death. Four Quartets seems to reenact the same process, most of all in the second and fourth movements of Little Gidding. Yet the drafts of the Quartets, and especially the drafts of those two movements, show the process being reenacted not out of urgent personal necessity, but from the head and as the working out of an idea . . . . The truth of The Waste Land is primary: whatever its larger cultural and human significance, it is rooted in and empowered by immediate experience and psychic energies. Is it the case that in the end the truth of Four Quartets is rather of a secondary sort: the product of thought more than experience; and a matter of congruence with a governing idea, and internal self consistency?*[123]

Well, is it? In court, we would object that the critic leads the witness. Rather than stating the opinion that the truth of Four Quartets is of a secondary sort, he frames it as a question and drops it on the reader.

Moreover, we must ask the meaning of the critic's primary-secondary distinction. In Freudian terms, a primary process is the undifferentiated physiological-psychological emotional reaction of the id. A secondary process differentiates inner from outer, me from not me, wish from fulfillment. A secondary process is of the ego. In this regard, The Waste Land is no more a product of a primary process than Little Gidding. All art consists in transforming raw material (emotions, primary process) into a finished product (poem, secondary process). The reader must decide for him or herself whether Eliot's religious concerns (I assume that is the "governing idea" at issue) provide a prearranged thought pattern that allowed him to write "from the head" and not from "urgent personal necessity," but in these considerations it is important to remember that The Waste Land was composed in the aftermath of a war and Little Gidding when the war was far from over. The crisis of The Waste Land is personal and psychical, that of Little Gidding is social and historic.

*   *   *

A more profitable way to look at the difference between the Waste Land and the Four Quartets is that of a public versus a private poem. A public poem has different concerns from one written to dramatize and express the poet's diseased sensibility. We may imagine the difference in the terms of doctor and patient. The patient, as sufferer, groans out his pain and his symptoms. The doctor has the tools and skills to turn this litany into a diagnosis and treatment plan. The doctor is not immune to the burden of illness (he is as prone to sickness as anyone), but his authority consists in his ability to recognize the nature of the disease and to chart the path to its arrest.

The question, then, is not whether Waste Land is a more personal statement of the poet's emotional state (a contest it would win if both poems were considered as private poetry), but, whether Eliot, in Four Quartets, provides therapy for what ails us. This, moreover, is not an historical question: we know the poem worked in its day. Rather, we must ask whether it still works for us today. This is the question of its enduring value.

*   *   *

191

That being said, it is undeniable the Four Quartets is more reflexive than The Waste Land, is not so nailed to the cross of the "horror." Though the newspapers of the 1920's were less charged with horrific events than those of the 1940's, we are faced with a chillier environment. The horror of The Waste Land is of the isolated individual who sees death and futility in the corner of his eye, no matter how he turns his head. When life is conceived as having a beginning at birth and ending in death, we alienate ourselves from the race and history. Then our life becomes a horror, an absurdity we cannot explain.

This is only the first movement of the spirit: renunciation. To embrace death is a good beginning, but is insufficient of itself.

The spirit must make a second movement envisioned in the opening of Little Gidding: the light shining on in the darkness that darkness cannot comprhend. In this movement, our lives are united with the lives of others. We are their continuation and they, ours. They light us to know ourselves and we cast the light by which they are known. The pattern of Four Quartets transcends the lone individual in the knowing that the individual and the race are one and the same, and the microcosm is the macrocosm.

*   *   *

We all begin in the raw egotism of the helpless infant. Our own needs, because we can do nothing of ourselves to fulfill them, are the most urgent things in our world. Our world begins in our elation at the fulfillment of our desires. Thus, patriotism begins in the conceit that *this* is the greatest country on Earth because *I* was born here. Only much later and after many tears does it become the best country on Earth because I have striven, whatever the cost, to make it so.

*   *   *

The muses, goddesses of the arts, were the daughters of Zeus and of Memory. Plato thought memory the source of virtue, as all learning is recollection. Jesus, on the night he was betrayed, instituted the sacrament of his body and blood, commanding his disciples to reenact it "in remembrance of me" (Luke 22.19). Dante's Comedy is one long, circular flashback, the entire journey represented as a memory. What is it about memory that it is extolled in myth, philosophy, religion and poetry?

If life is lived forward and understood backwards, how are we to choose in the present how we will live? There must be some pattern, some blueprint by which we choose ourselves. This is the use of memory in the transcending of desire, calling us into presence of a higher self.

We store, in memory, images of virtue that enable us to transcend momentary desire to grow in integrity. Memory bridges the chasm fixed between living and dead, for in enacting their virtue we give the dead new life.

*　　*　　*

Not the intense moment
Isolated, with no before and after,
But a lifetime burning in every moment
And not the lifetime of one man only
But of old stones that cannot be deciphered. (EC 192-196)

Eliot erred in Burnt Norton by trying to isolate timeless moments. Each time he remembered he remembered differently because between the memories he forgot. We construct each memory new each time we bring it to mind. The memory he invokes here is not a thing he makes, but the vision of the saints.

Love becomes liberation as it expands beyond the desire for satisfaction into the love of love for its own sake. Such a love forgets love of self and its satisfactions and offers itself to others. And the love of others loves, not what is *like* us, but what is unlike. For the love of like loves the mirror's image, confirming self-love. Only as we are liberated from the self can we accept what is and strive for what is best.

*　　*　　*

Sin is Behovely, but
All shall be well, and
All manner of thing shall be well.
If I think, again, of this place,
And of people, not wholly commendable,
Of no immediate kin or kindness,
But of some peculiar genius,
All touched by a common genius,
United in the strife which divided them;
If I think of a king at nightfall,
Of three men, and more, on the scaffold
And a few who died forgotten
In other places, here and abroad,
And of one who died blind and quiet
Why should we celebrate
These dead men more than the dying?
It is not to ring the bell backward
Nor is it an incantation
To summon the spectre of a Rose.
We cannot revive old factions
We cannot restore old policies
Or follow an antique drum.
These men, and those who opposed them
And those whom they opposed
Accept the constitution of silence
And are folded in a single party.
Whatever we inherit from the fortunate
We have taken from the defeated
What they had to leave us – a symbol:
A symbol perfected in death.
And all shall be well and
All manner of thing shall be well
By the purification of the motive
In the ground of our beseeching. (III.166-199)

Sin is behovely? How could Eliot, much less the medieval mystic, Dame Julian, whom here he quotes,[124] have missed the contradiction? Sin is not behovely, nor can it be. Sin is not nature but anti-nature. For a contradiction to become paradox, it must

194

be true when seen from the right *perspective*. Sin is behovely only *after* we have fallen into sin:

Our only health is the disease
If we obey the dying nurse
Whose constant care is not to please
But to remind of our, and Adam's curse,
And that, to be restored, our sickness must grow worse. (EC IV.152-156)

Sin is behovely (i.e. necessary) only after we have sinned (for it is only by a sin that sin enters our world), then sin becomes the ground of repentance, our only means of renewal. Taken in this way, it is also the ground of Dame Julian's confidence. In repentance and amendment of life all things will be well.

*   *   *

Dame Julian lived in a time of natural insults: she was felled when the great plague struck Europe. It was nearly as great a blood-letting as a world war, with an estimated quarter of Europe's population dead in four years. It spared Julian: she did not die, but returned from the dead to share her vision: all will be well.

*   *   *

Returning to Little Gidding and Mr. Every's play, we imagine the community receiving a king at its nightfall. If our vision broadens out beyond the drama, we see three men, Charles I, Laud and Strafford, awaiting death on the scaffold; Cranshaw, the Catholic, who died far from home; and Milton, who died blind and quiet. In life, these were men of every opinion and party.

"History," when it explains only what currently is, divides the dead into winners and losers, those worthy of remembrance and those who are not. But the dead, themselves, are united by the strife that bound them into a single party. Such "history," unfaithful to the dead, celebrates or forgets them. So

Eliot's reclaims a "small time, but greatly lived" that made no great splash in our world to be remembered.

*   *   *

Kierkegaard once claimed that the love of the dead is the most unselfish love,[125] because it is the love least likely to be repaid. Certainly, if it is mutual, the living are unaware of it. A parent's love for his child may, in a far off future be repaid, but more likely not. Suppose a parent knew that she would not be repaid? Would she spend as lavishly on her offspring, or would her love grow cold with reckonings of loss? Does she see love as a sacrifice or an investment? *What* is given does not matter (for one parent may give less but, by their manner of giving, give *more*) but *how* it is given is the test of love.

*   *   *

Eliot took care, in evoking the Seventeenth Century Civil War, to enclose the martial images within Dame Julian's feminine wisdom. He thus avoided a "romantic Bonnie Dundee period effect." Sir Walter Scott's song of Bonny Dundee goes:
'Come fill up my cup, come fill up my can,
Come saddle your horses, and call up your men;
Come open the West Port, and let me gang free,
And it's room for the bonnets of Bonny Dundee!"
Dundee he is mounted, he rides up the street,
The bells are rung backwards, the drums they are beat. [126]
Dundee rode into the teeth of history. In 1689 he fought the forces of William III at the behest of James II, dying in a lost cause.

The bells, rung backwards (that is, bass bell struck first and through to the treble, the reverse of the regular order) is a call to arms.[127] Eliot is emphatic here, we are not to ring the bell backward, nor follow an antique drum. Nostalgia won't do and trying to turn back the clock is pointless. The socio-political Rose of the Seventeenth Century is a ghost, not to be resuscitated. The

196

dead, moreover, in their single party, are, long since reconciled. Taking sides now would be folly.

*   *   *

Out here (in the graveyard), in fact, there is an attainment of what in life is vainly sought: equal distribution. Every family has a little piece of ground for itself, all about the same size. The view is about the same for all of them; no building rises so high that it takes away the sun's rays or the refreshing rain or the fresh air of the wind or the music of bird-song from a neighbor or the one across the way. No, here is equal distribution. In life it sometimes happens that a family which has lived in luxury and prosperity must cut back, but in death all of them have had to cut back. There can be only a slight difference – perhaps a foot in the size of the plot, or one family may have a tree, which other inhabitants do not have on their plots. Why do you suppose this difference exists? It is a profound jest to remind you by means of its littleness how great the difference was. How loving death is! For in this inspiring joke it is precisely death's love which with the help of this little difference reminds one of the great difference. Death does not say, "There is no difference at all"; it says, "There you can see what the difference was: half a foot."[128]

Kierkegaard sees in death a joke where Eliot sees a symbol. Death allows neither winners nor losers, princes nor paupers. Death makes all equal and worthy of remembrance. In thinking on the dead we purify our motive. If we imagine ourselves another's benefactor, in death, our beneficence is shown up for vanity: we have only shared what belongs to all. We possess only that we are allowed to take with us from this life and that is a place in the earth from which we came.

Movement No. 4

'Fare forward, you who think that you are voyaging;
You are not those who saw the harbour
Receding, or those who will disembark.
Here between the hither and the farther shore

While time is withdrawn, consider the future
And the past with an equal mind.
At the moment which is not of action or inaction
You can receive this: "on whatever sphere of being
The mind of a man may be intent
At the time of death" — that is the one action
(And the time of death is every moment)
Which shall fructify in the lives of others:
And do not think of the fruit of action.
Fare forward. (DS III.149-162)

We no longer need to supply Eliot the moment as we did in Burnt Norton. Here it is full and complete. Remember "will the climatis/stray down, bend to us; tendril and spray/ clutch and cling?" and the "kingfisher's wing" answering "light to light" (BN IV.129-135)? Does it not seem tame compared to:

The dove descending breaks the air
With flame of incandescent terror
Of which the tongues declare
The one discharge from sin and error.
The only hope, or else despair
Lies in the choice of pyre or pyre —
To be redeemed from fire by fire.

Who then devised the torment? Love.
Love is the unfamiliar Name
Behind the hands that wove
The intolerable shirt of flame
Which human power cannot remove.
We only live, only suspire
Consumed by either fire or fire.

Burnt Norton kept everything at a distance: the poet did not venture all on one throw. But that, the poet later realized, is what we do at every moment that we are not indifferent. The climatis does <u>not</u> stray down to us as we lay languid in our graves, but rather the dove descends, belching fire. Every moment is the moment of our death as, in the choosing, we are reborn.

*　　　*　　　*

198

Another contrast is with the fourth movement of the Dry Salvages. There the theophany is, by turns, merciful Mary and devouring Vishnu. Here the image is *simultaneous*. There is no lag between them: the Pentecostal dove dive bombs. We are trapped in the terrible realization that we are the target. We must choose, in the moment of our deaths, how we will understand it.

*   *   *

We must choose between famine and fast. In famine, we simply starve: we want but cannot eat due to a lack of food. We may fast, however, whether we have food or not. We would not eat, even if we had food, because food is not the focus of our intention, but the sacrifice. Either we see in the dove a threat to our physical lives or a spiritual trial enabling us to recognize our life has its purpose in transcending itself.

*   *   *

The fifth cantos of Inferno and Purgatorio mirror each other in their final characters: women caught in the act of adultery and murdered by enraged husbands. One, Francesca da Rimini, consigns her murderer to the deepest pit of Hell (Inferno 5.107). The other's (La Pia) place in Purgatory tells us she repented her sins in her final moments and forgave her husband (Purgatorio 5.133-136). As each died, one chose the sensual fires of lust (in Francesca's case, bloodlust) and the other the fire of charity and was forgiven as she forgave. The moments of their deaths are made eternal in the afterlife.

This is the choice of pyre or pyre: whether we, in our final moment (and the final moment is *every* moment) hold on to the fruit of action (Francesca (the stinging nettle)) or surrender it (La Pia (the dead nettle)) determines whether the "dark dove" flames with infernal or purgatorial fire.

*   *   *

To this point, Love has indeed been an "unfamiliar name." We were told that:

Love is itself unmoving,
Only the cause and end of movement,
Timeless, and undesiring
Except in the aspect of time
Caught in the form of limitation
Between un-being and being. (BN V.163.168)

Love is reduced to a metaphysical principle, an unmoved mover. In East Coker, the soul is advised to wait without love, for any object she chooses will be the *wrong* object (EC III.124-126): Love (along with faith and hope) are in the waiting. She is, further told that "love is most nearly itself, when here and now cease to matter" (EC V.200-201). The Dry Salvages tells us the saints differ from "most of us" for whom there is but the "distraction fit, lost in a shaft of sunlight" by "a lifetime's death in love" ((DS V.204-208), ridiculing Burnt Norton as, at the beginning of the movement, he ridiculed those who seek omens of the future. Finally, in the parable of the nettles we learned love liberates from the future and the past as it expands "beyond desire" (LG III.156-159).

Here, love ceases to be a principle and becomes a *name*. And whose name is it? The name of the deviser of the *torment*, the weaver of the intolerable shirt of flame that human power cannot remove. The name is left a periphrasis.

*   *   *

Among Ovid's tales of love gone awry he tells that of Hercules and Dejanira (Metamorphoses 9.89-272). They, returning from their wedding, found a river in flood. Hercules had no fear for his own safety but worried for his wife. Nessus, the centaur, volunteered to bear Dejanira across the torrent as Hercules swam. Hercules swiftly negotiated the rapids and, once across, heard his wife's screams: Nessus was running off with her. Hercules notched his bow and fired. The arrow, poisoned with Hydra's blood, found its target and Nessus lay dying.

But, as he died, he conceived his revenge. He told Dejanira, that his shirt, impregnated with the Hydra's deadly blood, was a love charm and offered it to her to atone for his rape attempt. Should Hercules' love fade, the shirt will relume it. Dejanira took the shirt and Nessus died.

Hercules went on adventures and rumors returned to Dejanira that he had fallen for the lovely Iole. Desperate, she first thought to murder the girl, but, remembering the shirt, sent it to him. Hercules wore it to make a sacrifice, but the flames of the altar activated the Hydra's blood. Flames roared through his bloodstream as he felled great trees and built his funeral pyre. He commanded Philoctetes (of later fame in the Trojan War) to use his unerring bow to set the pyre alight.

All the gods grieved the death of the hero, the mortal man on his way to Hades. But, Jove revealed his paternity: Hercules, as his son, was half a god. Only the mortal part he had received from his mother would descend among the dead: his immortal part would join them on Olympus.

Once again we bump into incarnation. Hercules' human nature suffers, dies and descends to Hades, while his divinity ascended to Olympus. Christ, taken from the Cross, descends among the dead retaining his divinity and leads many souls from darkness to light. This is the "impossible union" (Ds V.215-219) not even Dante, could transmute from a primary to a secondary process (Paradiso 33.127-145). In Christ, human suffering is made divine, liberating the soul from the burden of sin.

Movement No. 5.

As each prior quartet introduced a rose, in Little Gidding each rose has had its place. At the recapitulation, each rose is reintroduced in turn:
What we call the beginning is often the end
And to make and end is to make a beginning.
The end is where we start from. (V.214-216)

201

The finale of Little Gidding begins like East Coker, reminding us of the circle, ending at its beginning and the beginning at its end. The end is never as we supposed and that is how it begins. The beginning is where we started and that is how it ends. The cycles of time, of seasons, of the phases of life, end as they began, bringing childhood, adolescence, adulthood and senescence as moons wax and wane. There is a season and a time to every purpose under heaven.

Our care, paradoxically, is not to care. Not to cling to self, or things or persons for we can only love those things we are willing to surrender. Each ending becomes a new beginning as places and faces maintain their identities by shifting their shapes.

We cannot keep what we have, but we let go this particular form comforted in knowing that another awaits us. Thus we allow the world to turn and we with it, unresisting. Thus we may enjoy the rose of the senses.

And every phrase
And sentence that is right (where every word is at home,
Taking its place to support the others,
The word neither diffident nor ostentatious,
An easy commerce of the old and the new,
The common word exact without vulgarity,
The formal word precise but not pedantic,
The complete consort dancing together)
Every phrase and every sentence is an end and a beginning, (V.216-224)

If Four Quartets is a city of words, where the esoteric (haruspicate, scry, DS V.186) cohabits with the simon simple (dung, death EC I.46), there is no competition, though the words are, themselves, diverse. They are gathered and ordered so that each may contribute to the whole serving a purpose larger than itself.

*   *   *

In its depths I saw gathered together
And bound by love in a single volume that

Which, in the universe, are scattered leaves. (Paradiso 33.85-87)

Dante saw the universe bound together into a unity that leaves the parts no less real in individuality, but inseparable from the whole. A page torn from the book makes no sense on its own and the book, lacking the page, finds its meaning diminished. The pattern of the whole transcends a simple aggregation of parts. The whole consort, dancing together, means more than all the words separately. This is the socio-political Rose.

*   *   *

Every poem an epitaph. And any action
Is a step to the block, to the fire, down the sea's throat
Or to an illegible stone: and that is where we start.
We die with the dying:
See, they depart, and we go with them.
We are born with the dead:
See, they return, and bring us with them.
The moment of the rose and the moment of the yew-tree
Are of equal duration. A people without history
Is not redeemed from time, for history is a pattern
Of timeless moments. So, while the light fails
On a winter's afternoon, in a secluded chapel
History is now and England. (V. 225-237)

Every action is both ending and beginning. Every poem is an epitaph, complete in itself. Our every action follows Charles I to the block, sets alight the bombed city, sweeps the warriors down Vishnu's throat or glances at Nicholas Ferrer's headstone. This is not morbid, but results from a radical humility that reckons every moment as the moment of death.

The individual is the race and the race, the individual. We do not have our being in ourselves, but in relation to all previous generations. Those who come after us will not have their being except as they take us into account. The living are born in the several seasons, but the dead are a single "generation." The time of the dead and the time of the living, though one is short and the other long, are of equal duration.

*   *   *

Some wish to deny temporality, claiming inevitability as immunity to time. But coming to be is an agony. Existing is an agony. Ceasing to be is an agony. Agony is all, unless it is mirrored in an awareness and that awareness cannot be in time and hold an image. And awareness, while not located in time, must possess a vehicle in time. So, history is in a secluded chapel on a winter afternoon, or an upper room in Massachusetts, or wherever you are now.

*   *   *

With the drawing of this Love and the voice of this Calling

Quotations from two Fourteenth Century mystics, one male (the author the Cloud of Unknowing) and one female (Dame Julian), enclose the second part of the finale, but Dante, whose life spanned into the first quarter of the Fourteenth Century, has the final word.

*   *   *

Nan-in, a Japanese master duting the Meiji era (1868-1812), received a university professor who came to inquire about Zen.

Nan-in served tea. He poured his visitor's cup full, and then kept on pouring.

The professor watched the overflow until he could no longer restrain himself. "It is overfull. No more will go in."

"Like this cup," Nan-in said, "You are full of your own opinions and speculations. How can I show you Zen unless you first empty your cup?"[129]

The Cloud of Unknowing calls us out of the smug darkness of knowing into the dark cloud of unknowing, into the simple truth that we do not know God. Ignorance is the first step to knowing and knowing can only begin when we recognize that

204

we do not know. Love draws to forget what love is in order to learn anew, beginning an endless pursuit of knowledge attained through ignorance. This is humility: they who feed on the bread of angels ever hunger (Sirach 24.21).

*   *   *

We shall not cease from exploration
And the end of all our exploring
Will be to arrive where we started
And know the place for the first time. (V.239-243)
Where is there an end to it, the endless sailing, the dolorous lengthening of fruitless hours, in search of an island that is, perhaps, oceanless? While sea and land embrace amid the wreckage, of what we had once believed most admirable and, therefore, least likely of derivation?

We shall not cease exploration because human being is radically incomplete. Our salvation lies not in finding some "missing piece" of ourselves (like Aristophanes in Symposium), but in our constant return to the beginning, seeking ever from a new perspective. There is no end to the journey as there is no end to humility, for to be perpetually a beginner is to be alive.
Through the unknown, unremembered gate
When the last of earth left to discover
Is that which was the beginning;
At the source of the longest river
The voice of the hidden waterfall
And the children in the apple-tree
Not known, because not looked for
But heard, half-heard, in the stillness
Between two waves of the sea.
Quick now, here, now, always —
A condition of complete simplicity
(Costing not less than everything) (V.244-255)
And the return to Eden, at the source of the longest river, is not a regression, but progress. The first place has become the last left to discover. The cataract roars, plunging into nothingness as unborn children play in the apple tree. They are

205

not heard, above the commotion as eternity passes on silent feet. And the deceiving thrush delivers a truthful answer, eternity is here, now and always.

This simplicity costs more than money, but also secure doctrine, satisfaction and wisdom. The pilgrim has his begging bowl.

*   *   *

And all shall be well and
All manner of thing shall be well
When the tongues of flame are in-folded
Into the crowned knot of fire
And the fire and the rose are one. (V.256-260)
Dame Julian chimes with a final counsel of trust. And Dante contributes the final image:
The universal form of this knot
    I believe I saw because of
    The ample joy I feel in saying this, (Paradiso 33.91-93)
That universal knot is all things, substances, accidents and their relations, tied up into one, bound together by God, so that. as the knot binds three roses, the fire and the rose are one.

Notes

[1] Stephen Spender,T. S. Eliot, The Viking Press (New York, 1975) p. 1-2

[2] Soren Kierkegaard, Concluding Unscientific Postscript to the Philosophical Fragments, Howard V. and Edna H. Hong, trans., Princeton U Press (Princeton, NJ, 1992)

[3] For an account of this clash see Josef Pieper, Scholasticism: Personalities and Problems of Medieval Philosophy, Richard and Clara Winston, trs., St. Augustine's Press (South bend, IN, 2001) p. 121-126 or Richard E. Rubinstein, Aristotle's Children, Harcourt Inc. (Orlando, FL, 2003) p. 206-228

[4] Friedrich Nietzsche, Beyond Good and Evil, R. J. Hollingsdale, trans., Penguin Classics (London, 1993) p. 32

[5] Mark Lilla, The Stillborn God: Religion, Politics, and the Modern West (Vintage, 2008-09-23) Kindle Edition. p. 64-65

[6] Ludwig Wittgenstein, Culture and Value, Peter Winch, trans., U of Chicago Press (Chicago, 1984) p. 74e

[7] H. A. Nielsen, A Meeting of Minds on Water, in The Grammar of the Heart, Richard H. Bell, ed., Harper and Row (San Francisco, 1988) p. 77

[8] Rene Descartes, A Discourse of a Method of Rightly Conducting One's Reason and Seeking Truth in the Sciences, in Descartes: Selected Philosophical Writings, John Cottingham and Robert Stoothoff, trans., Cambridge U Press (Cambridge, UK, 1988) p. 47

[9] Lyndall Gordon, T. S. Eliot: An Imperfect Life, W. W. Norton & Company (New York, 1998) p. 353

[10] A. David Moody, Four Quartets: Music, Word Meaning and Value, in The Cambridge Companion to T. S. Eliot, A David Moody, ed., Cambridge U Press (Cambridge, UK, 2006) p. 142-43 details the various dates of publication.

[11] Helen Gardner, The Composition of the Four Quartets, Oxford U Press (New York, 1978) p. 26 the quote is from a letter Eliot wrote to John Heyward in 1942

[12] Ludwig Wittgenstein, Tractatus Logico-Philosophicus, D. F. Pears & B. F. McGuiness, trans., Routledge & Kegan Paul (London, 1963) p. 147, 6.4311

[13] Eliot, On Poetry, p. 21

[14] Wittgenstein, Tractatus, p. 151, 6.53

[15] Eliot, Essays, p. 124-125

[16] Moody, Quartets, p. 148-149

[17] Eliot, Essays, p, 218-219

[18] C. S. Lewis, The Discarded Image: An Introduction to Medieval and Renaissance Literature, Cambridge U Press (Cambridge, UK, 2006) just giving Lewis credit for the theft of his title.

[19] A. David Moody, Thomas Stearns Eliot: Poet, Cambridge U Press, (Cambridge, UK, 1991) p. 198

[20] Friedrich Nietzsche, The Gay Science, Walter Kaufmann, trans., Vintage Books (New York, 1974) p. 273 #341

[21] Alison Cornish, Reading Dante's Stars, Yale U Press (New Haven, CT, 2000) p. 136 This is heavy-duty Medieval philosophy with Thomas Aquinas and Augustine of Hippo both weighing in on a conversation with Dante eavesdropping.

[22] T. S. Eliot, The Family Reunion, in Complete Poems and Plays, Harcourt, Brace & Company (New York, 1980) Part II scene II, p. 272

[23] Soren Kierkegaard, Papers and Journals: A Selection, Alistair Hannay, ed. Trans, Penguin Classics (London, 1996) p. 161 43 IV A 164

[24] Soren Kierkegaard, The Concept of Anxiety, Reidar Thomte, trans., Princeton U. Press (Princeton, NJ, 1980) p. 10

[25] A. David Moody, Thomas Stearns Eliot: Poet, Cambridge U Press, (Cambridge, UK, 1991) p. M

[26] Eliot, Essays. P. 269

[27] Jean Jacques Rousseau, Emile or on Education, Allan Bloom, tr., BasicBooks (New York, 1979) p. 358

[28] Gordon, Life, p. 294 "Vivienne was Eliot's muse only so long as he shared her Hell."

[29] Gardner, Composition, p. 83, of course the ghosts in the first garden could be merely the adults watching over exploring children, but who would advocate so prosaic an interpretation?

[30] Kramer, Time, p. 38

[31] Soren Kierkegaard, The Concept of Anxiety, Reidat Thomte, trans., Princeton U Press (Princeton, NJ, 1980) p. 185 V B 53:11 "If anyone wishing to instruct me should say, "consistent with the preceding you of course, could say, 'It (the serpent) is language,' " I would reply, "I did not say that."

[32] Cleo McNelly Kearns, T. S. Eliot and Indic Traditions: A Study in Poetry and Belief, Cambridge U Press (Cambridge, UK, 1987) p. 232

[33] T. S. Eliot, Murder in the Cathedral, in Complete Poems and Plays, Part II, p. 209

[34] Gardner, Composition, p. 38

[35] Nietzsche, Gay Science, p. 225-226 #279

[36] Ananda Coomaraswamy, Buddha and the Gospel of Buddhism, Citadel Press (Secaucus, NJ, 1988) p. 39-40

[37] Gardner, Composition, p. 33-34

[38] Gardner, Composition, p. 38

[39] Wittgenstein, Tractatus, p. 151 7

[40] Wittgenstein, Tractatus, p. 149 6.44

[41] Moody, Eliot, p. 194

[42] Arthur Koestler, the Ghost in the Machine, Picador (London, 1975) p. 272ff.

[43] Moody, Eliot, p. 203

[44] Moody, Eliot, p. 206

[45] Moody, Eliot, p. 242

[46] Gordon, Life, p. 15

[47] Gardner, Composition, p. 99

[48] Gordon, Life, p. 17

[49] Kramer, Time, p. 77

[50] Eliot, On Poetry, p. 159

[51] Saint John of the Cross, Ascent of Mount Carmel - Enhanced Version, E. Allison Peers, trans.(2010-07-27).. Christian Classics Ethereal Library. Kindle Edition. (p. 35)Book 1 Chapter 13. 11

[52] Gerd Brand, The Essential Wittgenstein, Robert E. Innis, trans., Basic Books (New York, 1979) p. 85

[53] Kramer, Time, p. 94

[54] Moody, Eliot, p. 219

[55] Gardner, Composition, p. 108, Hayward pointed out that Eliot's conception had its roots in Sir Thomas Browne. Gardner, here, quotes him ("For the world, I count not an Inn, but an hospital, and a place, not to live in, but die in.").

[56] Gardner, Composition, p. 44 Preston, interpreting the lyric, originally thought as I do, that Satan is the "ruined millionaire," he thanks Mr. Eliot for disabusing him of the notion. Interestingly, Gardner disagrees and, as I do, offers a different interpretation.

[57] Eliot, Essays, p. 212

[58] Garder, Composition, p. 4

[59] Kenneth Page Kramer, Redeeming Time: T. S. Eliot's Four Quartets, Cowley Press (Plymouth, UK, 2007) p. 100

[60] Eric Sigg, Eliot as a Product of America, in the Cambridge Companion to T. S. Eliot, Cambridge U Press (Cambridge, 2006) p. 15

[61] Eliot, Criticize, p. 51

[62] Eliot, Criticize, p. 44

63 Spender, Eliot, p. 18

64 Spender, Eliot, p. 16

65 Gardner, Composition, p. 48

66 Derek Traversi, T. S. Eliot: The Longer Poems, Harcourt, Brace and Jovanovich (New York, 1976) p. 152

67 Kramer, Time, p. 240 n. 7

68 Gardner, Composition, p. 4, n. 3 Dame Helen characterized the wide currency of this article as "unfortunate."

69 Gardiner, Composition, p. 120

70 Gardner, Composition, p.120 n. 1

71 Gardner, Composition, p. 52

72 Gardner, Composition, p. 53

73 Gardner, Composition, p. 49

74 Gardner, Composition, p. 48-49

75 Sigg, American, p. 23-24

76 T. S. Eliot, The Use of Poetry & the Use of Criticism, Harvard U Press (Cambridge, MA, 1961) p. 70

77 Gardner, Composition, p. 128

78 Traversi, Poems, p. 159

79 Gardner, Composition, p. 133

80 Wittgenstein, Tractatus, p. 151 6.54

81 Soren Kierkegaard, Concluding Unscientific Postscript to the Philosophical Fragements, Howard H. and Edna V. Hong, trans., Princeton U Press (Princeton, NJ, 1992) p. 201

82 Peter S. Hawkins, Dante's Testaments: Essays in Scriptural Imagination, Stanford U Press (Stanford, CA, 1999)

83 Contra Wittgenstein, Tractatus, p. 145 #6.41

84 Gardner, Composition, p. 54

85 Kramer, Time, p. 245 n. 23

86 Martin Luther, Commentary on the Epistle to the Galatians, *www.studylite.org/com/mlg, Comments on Gal. 4.8*

87Kearns, Indic, p.133-134

88 Friedrich Nietzsche, *The Antichrist*, in *The Portable Nietzsche*, Walter Kaufmann, trans., Penguin Books (New York, 1976) p. 582 #16

89 Eliot, Essays, p. 219

90 Mohandas K. Gandhi, The Bhagavad Gita According to Gandhi, Mahatma Random House Inc Clients, 2010. Kindle Edition.

91 Kearns, Indic, p. 249

92 Wittgenstein, Tractatus, p. 147 #6.43

93 Moody, Eliot, p.231

[94] Gardner, Composition, p. 138

[95] Eliot, Murder, p. 191

[96] Gandhi, Bhagavad Gita,

[97] Ghandi, Bhagavad Gita,

[98] Kearns, Indic, p. 248

[99] Gardner, Composition, p. 34

[100] Moody, Eliot, p. 232f.

[101] Gardner, Composition, p. 141

[102] Kearns, Indic, p. 251-252

[103] Soren Kierkegaard, Sickness Unto Death, Howard V. and Edna H. Hong, trans., Princeton U Press (Princeton, NJ, 1980) p. 13

[104] Kramer, Time, p. 255 n.51, Kramer disagrees

[105] Friedrich Nietzsche, Thus Spake Zarathustra, in The Portable Nietzsche, Walter Kaufmann, trans., Penguin Books (New York, 1976) p. 198, 2.2

[106] Nietzsche, Zarathustra, p. 137

[107] Traversi, Poems, p.

[108] Moody, Eliot p. 333

[109] Gardner, Composition, p. 163

[110] Kearns, Indic, p. 256

[111] Gardner, Composition, p. 137

[112] Gardner, Composition, p. 141

[113] Eliot, Essays, p. 213

[114] T. S. Eliot, What Dante Means to Me, in The Poet's Dante, Peter S. Hawkins and Rachel Jacoff, ed., Farrar, Strauss and Giroux (New York, 2001) p. 32

[115] Moody, Eliot, p. 248

[116] Dante Aligheri, The Divine comedy of Dante Aligheri: Inferno, Ronald Martinez and Robert Durling, trans., Oxford U Press (New York, 1996) p. 245 notes on Inferno 15.124

[117] Moody, Eliot, p. 249

[118] Gardner, Composition, p. 64, 174

[119] Gardner, Composition, p. 64f.

[120] Gardiner, Composition, p. 188, Eliot had originally written "buried" but finding it too biographical a detail, struck it out.

[121] Moody, Eliot, p. 250

[122] Gardner, Composition, p.228f.

[123] Moody, Eliot, p. 327

[124] Moody, Eliot, p. 370 n. 68

[125] Soren Kierkegaard, Works of Love, Howard and Edna Hong, trans., Harper Touchbooks (New York, 1962) p. 322
[126] Gardner, Composition, p. 70
[127] Gardner, Composition, p. 204f.
[128] Kierkegaard, Works, p. 318
[129] Reps, Zen, p. 5

Made in the USA
Middletown, DE
25 April 2021

38422625R00119